ROYALTY IN THE AQUARIUM: THE MARINE ANGELFISHES

Acquisition, Care and Pair Formation
by Joachim Frische

A QUARTERLY

yearBOOKS, INC.

Dr. Herbert R. Axelrod,
Founder & Chairman

Neal Pronek
Chief Editor

Dr. W.E. Burgess
Editor

yearBOOKS are all photo composed, color separated and designed on Scitex equipment in Neptune, N.J. with the following staff:

DIGITAL PRE-PRESS
Patricia Northrup
Supervisor
Robert Onyrscuk
Jose Reyes

COMPUTER ART
Patti Escabi
Sandra Taylor Gale
Candida Moreira
Joanne Muzyka
Francine Shulman

Advertising Sales
George Campbell
National Advertising Manager
Amy Manning
Advertising Director
Sandy Cutillo
Advertising Coordinator
Nancy Sabina Rivadeneira
Periodical Advertising Manager
Cheryl Blyth
Periodicals Sales Representative
Julie Shernius
Sales Coordinator

©yearBOOKS,Inc.
1 TFH Plaza
Neptune, N.J. 07753
Completely manufactured in
Neptune, N.J.
USA

PREFACE

Marine angelfishes have been favorites of marine aquarists from the very beginning of the hobby. The common names of many of them testify to the high esteem in which they are held — Emperor Angelfish, Queen Angelfish, Regal Angelfish, etc.—and in Germany all of them are called Kaiserfische (= Emperor Fishes). Few other fish groups rival the appeal of their brilliant colors, attractive shapes, and fascinating behaviors. In spite of their great attraction to marine hobbyists, there probably has been less success proportionately in their keeping than in most other popular marine aquarium fish groups. Some of these failures have, of course, been due to the inherent delicacy of a number of the species or the impossible demands they make upon the aquarist regarding their diets. Much of the problem, however, has been due to the lack of knowledge of the techniques of keeping these fishes. Joachim Frische has in this book advanced the knowledge and techniques of keeping marine angelfishes to a point where greater success is assured. It can be seen from his writing that he cares a great deal about the "Kaiserfische" and is trying his best to see to it that they are cared for in such a manner that they can be expected to live many years in captivity, giving their owners much pleasure and satisfaction. His vast experience with these fishes is very evident as he describes their needs with regard to both their environment and their diet.

You cannot just dump any angelfish into any tank and expect success. According to the author you must know how large a tank is needed and what decorations should be included. If a reef tank is to be used, one must know what invertebrates can coexist with the angelfishes and which ones will be looked upon as food. And that's not all. One must know their social interrelationships so that more than one individual may be kept in an aquarium without them killing one another. Not only must one know what these fishes eat in nature and what can be used as substitutes in aquaria, but also how to feed them and what to do if the angelfishes go on a hunger strike, a not uncommon event.

All these aspects of the keeping of marine angelfishes are treated by Joachim Frische in this book and will enable the reader to have reasonable expectations of success if the procedures outlined for genera and species are followed.

Warren E. Burgess

What are Quarterlies?

Books, the usual way information of this sort is transmitted, can be too slow. Sometimes by the time a book is written and published, the material contained therein is a year or two old...and no new material has been added during that time. Only a book in a magazine form can bring breaking stories and current information. A magazine is streamlined in production, so we have adopted certain magazine publishing techniques in the creation of this Quarterly. Magazines also can be much cheaper than books because they are supported by advertising. To combine these assets into a great publication, we issued this Quarterly in both magazine and book format at different prices.

CONTENTS

Classification - Page 5

**Acquisition, Acclimatization,
and Diseases - Page 7**

Forming Communities - Page 13

Centropyge - Page 15

Genicanthus - Page 27

Chaetodontoplus - Page 31

Apolemichthys - Page 36

Holacanthus - Page 40

Euxiphipops - Page 46

Pomacanthus - Page 46

Pygoplites - Page 59

FOREWORD

The marine angelfishes!

These fascinating beauties, whose graceful swimming and interesting behavior in the aquarium as on the reef make it unmistakably clear why they have been dubbed with royal names as emperor, king, or queen. Frequently, just a glimpse of these monarchs of the reef awakens the desire in people to have them in a marine aquarium at home. But most people, especially those who have not had the slightest experience with marine aquaria, seldom think about the problems involved in the care of these fishes.

The members of the family Pomacanthidae, the family to which these marine angelfishes belong, are definitely not for beginners! They are very particular as to water quality, food, and aquarium environment. The owner of such fishes, however, usually learns how to satisfy these demands through experience if he has no access to professional help, to tips through conversations with other aquarists, or to the pertinent literature.

A novice in the realm of marine aquaristics should first gain experience with reef-dwellers that are easy to care for. Here, one can choose from among many reef fishes. The exceptions, however, prove the rule and you hear again and again about beginners who raise "difficult" marine angelfishes successfully. Indeed, the role of "beginner's luck" should not be underestimated; but do not count on it—it happens only in exceptional cases!

The promise of success lies in the experience gained over time through intensive involvement with your pets and patience in confronting their ways of life. Remember that with each fish you acquire, be it a demoiselle or an angelfish, you are taking on responsibility for its appropriate care and, in fact, its life!

The purpose of this book is to share my years of experience in the care of marine angelfishes in both fish-only and reef aquaria with all those who are already caring for these monarchs of the reef and with those who would like to do so in the future. People who now have marine angelfishes will find in this book a supplement to literature that has already appeared. For those, however, who would like to keep these beautifully colored fishes in the future, this book is a passing on of the experience I have been able to

Joachim Frische.

acquire through years of the successful care of these animals. It should be noted that there is no substitute for personal, practical experience in caring for tropical marine animals.

I would be pleased and consider the book successful if, by the time you have finished reading it, you have gained useful information about marine angelfishes—information that will lead to a long and healthy life for these aquarium animals and that will enhance your understanding of their natural habitat. Only precise knowledge of their modes of life make it possible for us to care for animals in ways appropriate to their species, and this should be the goal for all of us.

Joachim Frische, Penzberg

ACKNOWLEDGMENTS

I would like to thank everyone who helped this book along its way from inception to reality.

First and foremost, I would like to thank T. F. H. Publications, Inc., for making possible the publication of this book. In particular I thank Mrs. Mary E. Sweeney, Dr. Warren E. Burgess, and Dr. Herbert R. Axelrod.

I am especially grateful to my wife Claudia, who listened to the text countless times in order to criticize and correct it.

I also thank Herbert Finck, Arnd Roediger, Dr. John E. Randall, Klaus Schatz, and Günter Spies for the illustrations they placed at my disposal.

The following have also earned my gratitude for valuable information on marine angelfishes and the correspondence entailed in obtaining it: Dr. Gerald R. Allen, Dr. Lev Fishelson, Dr. John E. Randall, and Dr. Ronald E. Thresher.

And I must not forget my in-laws, Waltraud and Friedrich Lissner, and the Werner Marx family, who were always willing to take care of my aquaria in a professional way during my absences.

DEDICATION:

I would like to dedicate this book to Helen and Jack Randall, who, through their tireless work in the field of ichthyology, are constantly discovering and describing new species and making them known to the public in their many publications.

Their knowledge is of great importance to the field of marine aquaristics.

CLASSIFICATION

The subjects of classification and specific differentiating characters of the individual genera and subgenera will not be treated here in detail. These are matters best left to the scientists. I present here only those general characteristics that make possible the identification of marine angelfishes that are useful to marine aquarists.

Marine angelfishes belong to the family known scientifically as Pomacanthidae. The family is further divided into anywhere from seven to eleven genera, depending upon which classification you adopt.

The genus *Pomacanthus* comprises three subgenera, *Euxiphipops*, *Pomacanthodes*, and *Pomacanthus*, in one classification, with the formerly recognized genus *Arusetta* assigned as a synonym of the subgenus *Pomacanthus*. In another classification scheme *Pomacanthus*, *Euxiphipops*, and *Arusetta* are all valid genera.

The genus *Centropyge* comprises three subgenera, *Centropyge*, *Paracentropyge*, and *Xiphipops* in one classification scheme, whereas *Centropyge* and *Paracentropyge* are valid genera in another.

The genus *Holacanthus* includes *Angelichthys*, *Holacanthus*, *Sumireyakko*, and *Plitops* as subgenera in one scheme, and *Holacanthus* and *Sumireyakko* as full genera in another.

The other genera recognized (without subgenera) are *Apolemichthys*, *Chaetodontoplus*, *Genicanthus*, and *Pygoplites*, although *Apolemichthys* has at times been considered a subgenus of *Holacanthus*.

To date, there are about 76 known species of marine angelfishes.

Centropyge bicolor. Photo by John O'Malley.

Apolemichthys xanthurus. Photo by John O'Malley.

Genicanthus watanabei female. Photo by John O'Malley.

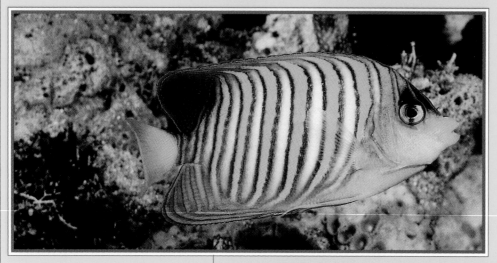

Pygoplites diacanthus.
Photo by John
O'Malley.

The differences between the various genera that should concern marine aquarists have mostly to do with size and shape. As usual, there are also transitional forms whose size and shape are not diagnostic for its genus. In such ambiguous situations, the structure of the opercular bones can be the "key to success." To illustrate this feature, diagrams of the opercular structure of five species are included. The information presented here will, in the majority of cases, enable marine aquarists to assign their newly acquired angelfishes to the correct genus.

Because this book describes the care of these fishes genus by genus, it offers the possibility of appropriate care even when there is no information about the actual species in question.

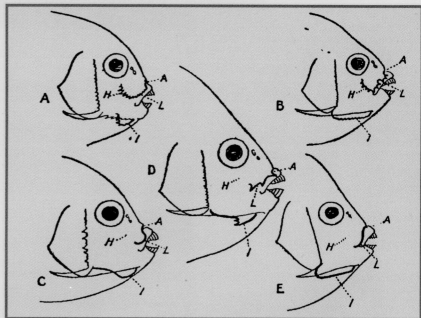

Form of preorbital and interopercular bones in: A. *Centropyge.* **B.** *Genicanthus.* **C.** *Pygoplites.* **D.** *Holacanthus.* **E. Other genera. A=Anterior. L=Lower. H=Hind margin of preorbital. I=Interoperculum.**

Pomacanthus maculosus. Photo by John O'Malley.

ACQUISITION, ACCLIMATIZATION, AND DISEASES

If you have decided to keep marine angelfishes in your aquarium, whether the dwarf or large species, you should pay attention to the following criteria at the time of purchase:

When buying large marine angelfishes, meaning for the most part species of *Pomacanthus* and *Holacanthus*, I most emphatically recommend getting young animals—still in their juvenile coloration if possible. In the vast majority of cases juvenile large angelfishes are still very adaptable and do not yet show the specializations of their adult counterparts. This means that there is usually no problem with acceptance of food substitutes in the aquarium, even in reef aquaria that contain many invertebrates; the sessile inhabitants are usually left in peace.

Full-grown specimens of a species or specimens in adult coloration frequently present feeding problems and often eat sessile invertebrates, especially if they are species that occur in the fishes' natural habitat.

An aquarium large enough to accommodate a full-grown marine angelfish in anything like an appropriate manner should hold about 520 gallons. Few aquarists have tanks of this size at their disposal. It goes without saying, then, that the size of the aquarium determines the size of the fishes you can acquire. As a rule, young marine angelfishes adapt their growth to the size of the space available, which means that even a young large marine angelfish can be kept quite nicely in a smaller aquarium, provided it holds no less than 100 gallons.

Although it is true that large marine angelfishes require rather large aquaria for proper care, the

A subadult *Holacanthus ciliaris*. It is best to purchase young angelfishes that are still in their juvenile coloration. Photo by Joachim Frische.

An adult *Pomacanthus asfur* in a reef aquarium. Photo by Joachim Frische.

space problem is easier to solve for dwarf or pygmy angelfishes. An aquarist can house these fishes appropriately in tanks holding 50 to 80 gallons. And dwarf angelfishes have another advantage. They can be kept extremely successfully with sessile invertebrates, for they hardly ever nibble on such tankmates.

The genera of marine angelfishes not yet mentioned constitute borderline cases, for the sizes of individual species of a genus may differ considerably. I recommend, then, as a rule of thumb, that you choose aquaria with capacities of at least 100 to 180 gallons.

Another point to observe when acquiring marine angelfishes is the exterior condition of the animal. If the fish has a sharply pointed back, often called a knife-back or razor-back, you can

conclude that it has not eaten in a long time. It is then question-able whether it will accept any substitute food at all, and, if it does, whether it will be able to make use of it, for after long periods of fasting the bacterial fauna of the stomach and intes-tine has frequently suffered irreversible damage. On this point the young fishes so suitable for aquaria are particularly demanding, for within a period of fourteen days they can become so emaciated that they scarcely have the energy to process the food they have eaten. In any event, I recommend that a feeding be requested while still at the dealer's tanks to determine whether the fish can eat at all. Moreover, such a test feeding should be done as a matter of course, because fishes that pass a visual inspection are not necessarily going to accept food.

But why would a fish refuse food? One reason may be that the fish is a feeding specialist, as is the case with many butterflyfishes or *Pygoplites diacanthus*. The animals are specialized feeders on certain polyps of one species of coral and refuse any other kind of food.

Another reason is that the fish is not at ease, because of lack of hiding places, for example, or because other inhabitants of the aquarium are harassing it. It may also be that the food is too large or too inappropriate. Remember, in all likelihood the food being offered is foreign to the fish, which has to get used to it before it can eat it. Yet another reason may be the mode of eating itself: a bottom fish, for example, must first learn how to take food from open water.

And now, back to the marine angelfishes, for which, apart from

Pygoplites diacanthus **is a feeding specialist and will not do well unless it is provided with its particular diet items. Photo by Roger Steene.**

very large animals, feeding is not likely to be much of a problem. If these fishes are kept in a "natural" aquarium inhabited by a number of sessile invertebrates, feeding problems are the exception, not the rule.

If you have decided to buy marine angelfishes, they will be netted from the tank at the retail outlet of a dealer and probably packed in plastic bags placed in a paper-lined shipping package, which, after the addition of oxygen, is sealed. The plastic bags are usually doubled to make it watertight in the event that the angelfish bites through one of them or pierces it with its spines. The paper used for lining, usually a newspaper, helps calm the fish because it darkens the transport bag and also provides insulation to prevent sudden temperature changes.

Once the fishes arrive at your home, transfer them carefully to a suitable container and begin to exchange the bag water for aquarium water; keep this up until 70% of the water in the container is from the aquarium. The easiest way to do this is with a plastic tube: let the aquarium water flow into the container drop by drop. This method, known as the "drip method" of adaptation to the aquarium water is infinitely preferable to the "dump-it-in method" because it gives the fishes a chance to adjust slowly to the new water conditions.

Once the water is equalized, the marine angelfishes are released into their new home. But how should an aquarium for marine angelfishes be set up?

The best aquarium to use is one set up as a reef aquarium. In it, the fishes will find the many hiding places they so urgently need. Furthermore, it is a natural environment that offers first foods in the form of small crustaceans and delicate algal growths.

If such an aquarium is not available to you, at least use one with many hiding places, and one that is well planted with species

of the algal genus *Caulerpa*. Algae are indispensable for the long-term care of any species of marine angelfish and is essential for vitality. Invariably, it is the first food taken in the aquarium. For many fishes, algae also play an important role in digestion, for they not only function as bulk but contain a number of vitamins important for the long life of your fishes.

Even though your fish took food at the dealer's establishment, it would not be unusual if it did not eat during its first few days at home; it first has to adjust to the new environment and new tankmates. However, if a fish that has accepted food in the dealer's tanks continues to refuse it at home—behavior frequently observed in adult marine angelfishes, it is important to have several kinds of food on hand; you will have to try them out one after another. Successful foods are those that are attractively colored, such as bloodworms, or new to the fish, such as flake and tablet food.

Marine angelfishes are territorial. This means that newly acquired animals often move slowly in the aquarium, carefully checking out hollows and niches, always on the lookout for an attacking member of its own species. If you plan to keep several animals, and most of us do, you must place several individuals of one species in the tank at the same time. This subject will be discussed in more detail in the chapter on pair formation. Not until it is sure that there are no rivals in the tank does the marine angelfish begin to swim confidently around the aquarium, finally looking for something to eat.

Once a new fish eats and regains its full color, is comfortable, and shows it by swimming continuously around in the aquarium looking for food, the only things that may endanger its health (aside from mechanical breakdowns) are ecto– or en-

doparasites. The most well known of these are the pathogen *Cryptocarion irritans* and species of the genus *Oodinium*. But fungi and worms are also treacherous and can end the life of a fish very quickly.

But first, before I discuss ways to fight diseases successfully, a word on the origin of diseases. In natural environments, it is highly unlikely that a healthy, lively fish will become diseased, a situation due to the sheer vastness of its habitat and the stability of environmental conditions. Most pathogens have only one brief period of their reproductive cycle during which to locate a suitable fish host; because the ocean is so vast, the parasites seldom accomplish that goal and soon die.

What happens when the stable environment is perturbed? One example is the annual rainy season, when, within a short period of time, huge quantities of fresh water enter the ocean. As a result, many shore-dwelling fishes become diseased and the weakest animals die. When stable water values return, the fishes return to health and the parasitic attack disappears.

WHERE DO PARASITES COME FROM?

We are talking about minute organisms that are always to be found in the mucous membranes of fishes. Their only chance to reproduce, however, comes when something happens to the mucous membrane or the fish's vitality is reduced, which, of course, is what happens when the animal is caught and transported. The more frequently this occurs, the worse it is for the fish, and this is why a quarantine period at the dealer's establishment is so important. It is a time for the fish to calm down before it is passed on to an aquarist.

This latent infestation of parasites also explains why disease appears even though no new fish has been added to the

Many different remedies, preventives, and tonics are available at pet shops. Photo courtesy of Jungle Laboratories.

tank in several months. The parasites usually become active if the water quality is poor or if the fish is under the stress of continual harassment by other fishes. Too many fishes in the tank may, therefore, also be the cause of a sudden outbreak of disease.

The appearance of *Cryptocarion* or *Oodinium* is never exclusive. These are called "mixed" infections because along with the pathogen there is a bacterial infection of the skin.

Good living conditions in an aquarium are achieved through a well-functioning filtration system. And the main element of this is an excellent skimmer. The mechanical setup will be enhanced by a weekly water change, calibrated so that about 10% of the gross volume of the tank is exchanged every month.

Reef aquaria have been shown to forestall the circumstances I have described as contributing to the outbreak of a disease. In such aquaria, fishes are soon comfortable, and the problem of overpopulation is excluded because otherwise the invertebrates would die. And the invertebrates themselves contribute to a water quality that is only rarely achieved in a fish aquarium.

There is a problem, however, in keeping a combination of invertebrates and fishes: it is

difficult to cure the fishes with appropriate medication. There are a number of medications that make promises, but they do not always work.

UV lights can be used successfully, provided they are bright enough. An effective arrangement is to use two UV lights of at least 36 watts placed one directly behind the other; these should be left on continuously.

What do UV lights do? The principle behind UV lights is simply that they produce ultraviolet light, which either kills tiny

organisms or alters their genetic material to the point that they can no longer reproduce. The sun does the very same thing. This is why only a very small number of germs are found in surface waters of oceans: on the order of one germ colony per 2.6 gallons of water.

In the aquarium, this ratio is many times higher, which means that diseases spread more efficiently there than in the open ocean. Properly installed UV lights counter this problem quite effectively and are effective against various diseases. Of course, plankton is also destroyed, but a good reef aquarium produces a continuous, replenishing supply. Please note, however: Never shine UV light directly onto the water, because it will burn the fishes. In addition, it will damage the corneas of both fish and human eyes. Even people do not look at the sun without sunglasses or expose themselves to it without wearing sunscreen.

To supplement the UV lights you can also use a diatom filter, but only when there is a problem with disease, for diatom filters very quickly remove the plankton from the water.

Ozone generators are widely available and can be effective as destroyers of bacteria if common-sense precautions are taken during their use. Photo courtesy of Ultralife Reef Products.

If you set up a quarantine aquarium, you can give medications there that would otherwise be harmful to the invertebrates. But even a quarantine tank is no guarantee that the fishes, once cured, will not get sick again when they are put back into their old tank, because the cause of the problem may lie in poor water quality in the display tank. And even just the catching and moving of a fish may be enough to affect its health adversely, causing the disease to break out anew. Furthermore, quarantine aquaria, as a rule, contain only a bare minimum of furnishings and are sterile, situations that are not likely to contribute to a fish's well-being. Even treatment with medication entails stress, which could lead to the animal's refusal to eat and, ultimately, its death.

Experience has shown that preventive treatment with UV light is the most effective method and guarantees the greatest success, as long as the lights are installed and used correctly.

Now I will discuss a few diseases and possibilities for combating them. The diseases covered are only those that marine angelfishes are most prone to.

SUMMARY OF COMMON DISEASES AND POSSIBLE TREATMENTS

CRYPTOCARION IRRITANS (Marine Ich)

Diagnosis: white, pinpoint-size spots all over the body, fins, and eyes. The fish avoids hard objects. Attack often increases toward evening. Appears in new fishes frequently on the fourth day in their new home.

Contagious: Yes.

Treatment: 1. Copper sulfate: basic solution 1 g/l. Add 1.6 ml of this for each quart of aquarium water daily until the disease has disappeared; then do a 30% water change and filter through activated charcoal. During treatment, do not use activated charcoal, UV lights, or ozone.

2. Quinine hydrochloride or quinine sulfate: 1 g of this substance to 20-25 gallons of aquarium water; a 30% water change after two or three days. Repeat the dosage. Repeat the procedure as often as necessary until the disease has disappeared. Once the treatment is successful, do another 30% water change and filter with activated charcoal. During treatment, no activated charcoal, UV light, or ozone should be used.

THESE MEDICATIONS SHOULD BE USED ONLY IN QUARANTINE AQUARIA, BECAUSE THEY ARE HARMFUL TO THE INVERTEBRATES IN REEF AQUARIA.

GILL WORMS

Diagnosis: Fish shy away from decorations. Rapid breathing (!), indicated by how fast the gill covers are moving.

Contagious: No.

Treatment: Freshwater bath: Fill a suitable container with water, 10% marine and the rest fresh. Be very sure that the temperature is the same as that in the aquarium. Do not use distilled water. The worms die from pH and osmosis shock. Bathe for 15-30 minutes, watching the fish continuously. If the animal lies on its side or begins to roll, stop treatment immediately. If necessary, repeat the treatment a week later.

Commercial medications may be available in your area; check with your dealer.

LYMPHOCYSTITIS:

Diagnosis: White nodules of various size on skin and fins.

Contagious: No.

Treatment: None necessary; if water quality and living conditions are good, the nodules will go away by themselves in about two weeks.

OODINIUM OCELLATUM (Velvet Disease)

Diagnosis: Very small, white spots, increasing rapidly in number. As the disease progresses, the fish looks as if it is covered with powered sugar. The fish shy away from objects, remaining in the current, for they are suffering from acute shortness of breath (Oodinium also attacks the gills!). Refusal to eat.

Contagious: Yes.

Treatment: 1. Copper sulfate: basic solution 1 g/l. Add 1.6 ml to each quart of aquarium water daily until the spots have completely disappeared. Then do a 30% water change and filter through activated charcoal. During treatment, no activated charcoal, UV lights, or ozone should be used.

2. Quinine chloride or quinine sulfate: Add 1 g of this substance to 20-25 gallons of aquarium water. After two to three days, a 30% water change should be made. Repeat this procedure as often as necessary until the attack has disappeared completely. Then, a 30% water change and filtration through activated charcoal. During treatment, no activated charcoal, UV lights, or ozone should be used.

THESE MEDICATIONS SHOULD BE USED ONLY IN QUARANTINE AQUARIA, BECAUSE THE CHEMICALS ARE HARMFUL TO INVERTEBRATES AND PLANTS.

WHEN MEDICATION IS ADMINISTERED, IT IS CRITICAL TO FOLLOW DOSAGE INSTRUCTIONS.

A disastrous attack of Oodinium occurs when it attacks only the gills. The symptoms resemble those of gill worms, but treatment for that parasite does no good. If treatment for gill worms does not work, even after administered repeatedly, you are probably facing an attack of Oodinium.

POISONS AND POISONING:

1. Ammonia Poisoning (NH_3)

Diagnosis: Washed-out coloration, bulging eyes, possible dissolution of mucous membrane, areas of skin reddish underneath, apathetic behavior, rapid breathing, black spots that look like peppercorns.

Contagious: Does not apply.

Treatment: Immediate lowering of the pH value to below 7.5. At that point, the toxic ammonia changes to ammonium. After lowering the pH, transfer the fish to another aquarium in which the pH has also been lowered, for there is also ammonia in the fish's blood that must be excreted before the pH is raised again. The pH value is best lowered through a CO_2 adjustment, which is then reset to the original pH two or three days later. Keep the "old" aquarium in operation, performing a 30% water change. Shrimp and other invertebrates can remain in the aquarium because ammonia affects only red blood cells. Once nitrification bacteria have transformed the ammonia, the fishes can be put back. The cause of a rise in levels of ammonia is usually inadequate filtration and skimming in a tank holding too many fishes that are fed too much.

2. Nitrite Poisoning (NO_2)

Diagnosis: Fish's coloration fades. Fish wobbles and rolls. Later, affected fish will lie on the bottom, breathing heavily.

Contagious: Does not apply.

Treatment: Use ozone. Add between 10 and 20 mg per quart of aquarium water. Add it through the skimmer; putting it directly into the water burns the fish's skin. If ozone is not available, transfer the fish immediately to old, nitrite-free water. Do not use freshly made-up sea water. The causes are the same as in ammonia poisoning. The two poisonings usually appear in parallel.

In other cases, poisons may be carried through the air, when, for example, you are using solvents for carpet cleaning, painting, or wallpapering. Fumes are carried through the pump into the aquarium water and mixed in. If

Fluidized-bed canister filters are highly efficient at providing a large volume of biological filtration capacity by keeping the filter medium in constant motion. Photo courtesy of Red Sea Fish Pharmaceuticals

you are doing this kind of work in the room where the aquarium stands, it is critical to air the room out well and operate only the most essential pumps.

CONSTIPATION:

Diagnosis: Bloated body and red, swollen anal region. Fish does not eat.

Contagious: Does not apply.

Treatment: 1. Preventive measures: Add algae and vegetal food such as spinach and lettuce.

2. Administer Castor Oil: For large fishes only.

3. Freshwater bath: Fresh water with an additional 10% sea water. Do not use only fresh water. Duration—15 to 30 minutes. Usually osmotic shock will cause the fish to excrete wastes during its first 15 minutes in the bath. If the fish lies on its side or begins to roll, stop treatment immediately and repeat it the following day. Repeat the procedure if the first treatment is unsuccessful.

Artificial decorations in a tank housing marine Angelfishes should follow a marine theme in keeping with the nature of the aquarium. Photo courtesy of Blue Ribbon Pet Products.

FORMING A COMMUNITY TANK

The question of keeping marine angelfishes in a community tank has long been overlooked. There are two important aspects to consider: the problem of territorial behavior in many marine angelfishes, on the one hand, and, on the other, their feeding on sessile invertebrates kept in reef aquaria.

The second point will be treated specifically in the descriptions of individual species, but I should note here that, apart from the genus *Genicanthus*, all marine angelfishes now and then nibble on corals and other invertebrates—it is just part of their nature. And there are individual cases of *Pomacanthus* species, especially the larger ones, completely devouring invertebrates. Note first of all that stony corals, tridacnid clams, and many xeniids cannot be kept for long periods with marine angelfishes. If you are not prepared to give up keeping these invertebrates, do not take on the care of species of *Pomacanthus*.

You can counteract the territorial behavior of many marine angelfishes in a number of ways. Remember, however, that in nature the territory of some marine angelfishes of the genera *Holacanthus* or *Pomacanthus* may be a square mile or so, whereas dwarf or pygmy angelfishes of the genus *Centropyge* claim only a few coral heads. Only a few individuals of the same species live within the territory of a large angelfish, whereas several specimens of dwarf angelfishes may compete for a living within a small area. Territories are defended vigorously against intruders; members of other species are also attacked if their coloration is similar to that of the defender's species. First there are threats, followed by biting, and when this does not lead to the desired result the preopercular spines, which are quite effective weapons, are put to use. They seldom fail to make their point.

Aggression in marine angelfishes can be easily categorized. The more of a species there are in a territory, the weaker the aggressive behavior. In other words, large marine angelfishes occupying a large territory where few others of its species live are much more quarrelsome than dwarf angelfishes that share a small territory with several of their own species.

To insure preservation of the species, nature has provided juvenile large angelfishes with a different coloration, which protects them from aggression by adults. This makes it possible for young and old members of the same species to swim and feed peaceably together in the protection of the coral reef. But watch out! Juveniles of the same color, no matter what the species, are aggressive among themselves. This might not happen on the reef but can be fatal for weak individuals living in small aquaria. The sensible thing to do is to acquire one adult and one

A juvenile *Genicanthus lamarck*. The pattern of the caudal fin indicates that it is a female. Photo by Joachim Frische.

juvenile of a species that has different coloration at their respective stages.

But what happens when the juvenile begins to take on adult coloration? This situation is described at the end of this book, in the chapter on pair formation, for it plays an important role there.

For marine angelfishes that live in groups in small areas, the youngest animals are always the lowest in rank. If you are keeping these kinds of angelfishes, which include the genera *Centropyge* and *Genicanthus*, it is best to keep at least three individuals of a species. With dwarf angelfishes, be sure to put three different-sized fish into the aquarium at the same time, because similar sized individuals may harass one another, causing problems.

With species of *Genicanthus*, it is best to put one male and two or three females into the aquarium at the same time. Because the sexes are sexually dichromatic (having different coloration), telling them apart is easy.

In general, if the aquarist makes sure that the fishes he puts in with angelfishes are a different color or are larger, there will be no problem with a community tank.

If a marine angelfish has been showing aggressive behavior for a long time, it is important to provide an outlet for this aggression before it builds up to the point that it spills over onto other inhabitants of the aquarium that are simply bystanders. The ideal, but unattainable, solution would be to defuse aggression by having an intruder of the same species available. Since you cannot do this with a live animal, use a dummy or a mirror. Make the dummy out of wood and paint it the correct colors (using non-toxic waterproof paint of course).

Fasten it in position in the aquarium (monofilament works well); the movement of the water will make it appear to be alive, and the flesh-and-blood specimen will be stimulated to attack the intruder and drive it away.

The mirror method involves simply placing a mirror in the aquarium. The defender begins to attack the "intruder" incessantly, without realizing that it is waging a hopeless battle against itself. Be careful in choosing the mirror, for the reflecting layer may dissolve in sea water and toxify the aquarium.

These two effective and successful ways of handling aggression should be used once a month for two to three hours. They provide the fish with a change and, moreover, keep natural behaviors from atrophying. One more thing. The colors displayed by the finny fighter are astonishing!

Centropyge acanthops comes from East Africa. This is a 2 cm long juvenile. Photo by Joachim Frische.

GENUS: *CENTROPYGE*

We begin with the smallest members of the family Pomacanthidae, commonly referred to as dwarf or pygmy angelfishes and included in the genus *Centropyge*. Dwarf angelfishes are especially well suited for marine aquaria because many species do not grow larger than 5 to 6 inches. This makes them an ideal size for small aquaria holding about 50 or so gallons.

Another advantage of members of this genus is that they can be kept in a reef aquarium. Sessile invertebrates are, as a rule, not eaten, which does not mean, however, that the fish will not enjoy an occasional nibble on coral polyps or the mantle edges of a *Tridacna*. To think that you might be able to control this behavior is a pure waste of time, for it is innate and simply cannot be shut off. Consequently, you should not keep dwarf angelfishes if you cannot accept this situation.

The main food of dwarf angelfishes is algae. If you want to keep these fishes over the long term, you must also take this fact into consideration.

In addition to the advantages already mentioned, there is another thing to consider—the social behavior of many species of dwarf angelfishes. On the reef, many species live in a kind of harem. One male has several females, which themselves are subject to ranking within their group. The strongest female is ranked directly below the male. Then comes the second strongest female, and so on.

Because these dwarf angelfishes remain so small, it is naturally an advantage to get several individuals of one species and let the natural group

hierarchy develop in the aquarium. The animals will develop behaviors that never cease to fascinate their owner. It is important here that all individuals of one species be put in at the same time. It is also a good idea if the members of the group are all of different sizes. The advantage of these two bits of advice is that at the outset the fish do not have to fight to establish rank—it is simply determined by size.

A subadult *Centropyge acanthops*. This species is found at depths of up to 133 feet. Photo by Joachim Frische.

We have known for some time that many dwarf angelfishes can change their sex from female to male. This always happens when the group as a whole requires it. If the leader of the group, the male, is removed, the highest ranking female turns into a fully functional male in very short order. The rest of the females in the harem then move up a notch.

The aquarist can make use of this tendency if he is keeping one individual of a species of dwarf angelfish and wants to put in another one. Just make sure that

the new fish is smaller than the original inhabitant. As a rule, there is no problem. Harassment at the outset does not usually last very long, ceasing after a week or two.

In captivity, dwarf angelfishes have been seen to spawn in the evening, shortly before the lights are turned off. Now that reef aquaria are a part of marine aquaristics, it is relatively easy to get many kinds of fishes to spawn.

Chances are increased when blue-light bulbs are employed; when they alone are left on in the evening, they produce a quite natural dusky-blue atmosphere that induces many fish to spawn.

Although these fishes are small, you should not underestimate their territorial behavior toward other fishes, particularly toward fishes of similar size or coloration. Their preopercular spines serve as both offensive and defensive weapons—even fishes as small as dwarf angelfishes can wield them effectively.

All dwarf angelfishes do best in richly furnished aquaria that offer an abundance of caves, niches, and cracks. In nature, too, species of the genus *Centropyge* live in cavities among corals and rocks.

If you pay attention to such things, you will enjoy your dwarf angelfishes enormously, for they show themselves often, and their brilliant colors are impressive testimony that they, too, are royal fishes.

If you have now decided to get yourself some dwarf angelfishes, make sure to get young ones. You can tell how old a fish is by its size—the smaller it is the younger it is. In addition, some dwarf angelfishes have a juvenile stage. In general, animals measuring 1.2 to 2.4 inches are ideal for an aquarium. At this size they have no problem with acclimatization. They take almost any food you give them, but it should be as varied an assortment as possible. The following foods should always be on the menu: algae and frozen foods such as *Mysis, Artemia,* chirononid larvae, krill, fish eggs, plankton, and clams. They also take tablet and flake foods most readily. It seems pointless to mention that adaptation to aquarium life in a reef aquarium proceeds smoothly, whereas in a purely fish aquarium problems will crop up again and again.

To date, approximately 27 species of the genus *Centropyge* and 2 species of the genus *Paracentropyge* are known; these latter two species are not described here because they are not suitable for aquarium life—they do not accept a substitute diet.

Next, I will describe every species of *Centropyge* that is suitable for aquarium care, and that are relatively common in nature and easy to find at pet stores.

CENTROPYGE ACANTHOPS (NORMAN, 1922)

African Orange-backed Pygmy Angelfish

When dealers get a shipment from Kenya, small orange and blue dwarf angelfish turn up in the shops a short time later. This 2.8-inch-long fish is the African Orange-backed Pygmy Angelfish, *Centropyge acanthops.* Their range covers the reefs along the coastline of the southern part of the African continent, where they busily look for food at depths of up to 133 feet. They live out their lives mostly hidden among rocks and coral heads where their diet consists of small crustaceans and other invertebrates.

If an aquarist has satisfied his

Centropyge argi **comes from the Caribbean. It should be kept in the same manner as** *C. acanthops.* **Photo by Joachim Frische.**

urge to purchase some African Orange-backed Pygmy Angelfish and has furnished his aquarium in such a way that there are plenty of niches and caves, the acclimatization phase is relatively easy.

Reef aquaria filled with a variety of sessile invertebrates, or well-established aquaria with lots of algal growth are advantageous in caring for these fishes. I do not advise using aquaria that have been in operation only a

short time, for there will not be as many microorganisms present, and angelfishes that refuse food at first need these to feed on.

The first food that the African Orange-backed Pygmy Angelfish takes is usually small algae and crustaceans. They quickly accept a substitute diet, however, which should consist of *Mysis, Artemia,* and chironomid larvae.

With their bellies always turned toward the substrate, it is no wonder that these fish can look out of their cavity upside-down before leaving or disappearing into it. African Orange-backed Pygmy Angelfish are in constant motion—nothing deters them in their search for food. But they are careful not to spend too much time in open spaces.

In nature, *Centropyge acanthops* forms a harem consisting of one male and several ranked females; this arrangement is not only possible but also recommended for the aquarium, too. It may indeed happen that two animals of similar size will fight a little at first until they figure out who will lead the harem. Because, as mentioned in the description of the genus, many marine angelfishes can change sex, it is usually the case that the strongest fish is a male. The situation is serious if two fairly large individuals are in conflict, for eventually two rival males will stake out territories and the weaker one will probably die. This is the reason that it is very important to get small specimens, for they will probably all be females.

There are differences of opinion about the blue eye ring

that appears in many *Centropyge acanthops* individuals. Some see this eye ring as a sex-related character of females, whereas others maintain it is a regional color variant. Still others want to assign animals with eye rings to a new species or subspecies. Whatever the right view may be, one of these—the sex-specific theory—is justifiably doubtful. Observations in aquaria have shown that fish with eye rings mate with one another. The opposite situation has also been observed and documented.

Centropyge acanthops has already been induced to breed in aquaria several times. In a reef aquarium, it occurs at dusk and proceeds problem-free, usually in a rhythm of two to three days. Spawning occurs after the male has carefully nudged the female's belly several times with his snout. It looks as if he is trying to push her to the surface. Courtship coloration in males differs from the normal coloration in that the dark blue belly turns pale blue to almost white. Spawning behavior does not necessarily mean that spawning will actually happen. The male may have to make several attempts before his efforts are rewarded. Courtship coloration may also appear if animals are kept individually; at dusk, they may then court any fish at all—an unusual and certainly undesirable behavior.

Even though there are few problems nowadays in getting the fish to spawn in reef aquaria, raising the offspring is impossible because the food they require is not available in sufficient quantity. And it is not just food but other, still unknown factors, that make successful rearing difficult, putting the enthusiasm of the aquarist to the acid test. I do not advise isolating a mating pair, because, interestingly enough, it has been shown that they will promptly stop their spawning behavior. When the pair is put back into the community aquarium, it is not long before

spawning behavior can be observed once more. It appears as if the presence of other fishes is necessary for spawning to occur. The cause may lie in the higher level of stress, which, in nature, insures that the fish will get their spawning over quickly so that neither they nor their fertilized eggs will be eaten.

Because dwarf angelfishes, including *Centropyge acanthops*, are territorial, they instinctively defend their space. I refer to this behavior simply as aggression toward other fishes. Unfortunately, in *Centropyge acanthops* this behavior is quite pronounced, which means that, for example, you cannot add a *Centropyge*

In concluding this description, I should tell you that in a reef aquarium, *Centropyge acanthops* sometimes picks at soft corals of the family Xeniidae and may tear off a polyp or two in the process. If you have a special fondness for these sessile invertebrates and cannot tolerate their being eaten from time to time, you should not keep the African Orange-backed Pygmy Angelfish. Other sessile invertebrates are left alone. Among these are species of disk anemones, crustose anemones, gorgonians, soft corals, leather corals, and tube corals.

SUMMARY

Centropyge acanthops prefers

***Centropyge bicolor* is called the Blue-and-Gold Pygmy Angelfish for obvious reasons. Photo by Earl Kennedy.**

loriculus to the tank. The African Orange-backed Pygmy Angelfish will kill the weaker Flame Angelfish. The reverse situation, however, is also possible.

Basically, a *Centropyge acanthops* already in the tank tends to attack newly added fishes for two or three days before backing off and accepting them into the aquarium society. I recommend that all aquarium lights be turned off after new fish are introduced to initially give them a little peace. It is not a good idea to add other dwarf angelfishes.

aquaria with plenty of niches and caves to hide in. Highly recommended for the fish's well-being are crustaceans and algae.

Dwarf angelfishes are preferably kept in a reef aquarium—an aquarium holding a number of secondary invertebrate colonizers. In such a situation, the fish are easy to take care of, although it may happen that species of the family Xeniidae are damaged.

With regard to feeding, the obligatory frozen and dried foods are accepted.

To simulate a natural situation, it is best to get several individuals

A number of the essential oils and vitamins your fish need can be obtained from frozen, formulated foods. Photo courtesy of Biotope Research, Inc.

of one species at the same time, making sure that they are all of different sizes to avoid a later harassment problem.

In a reef aquarium, spawning is no problem. A pair forms within the harem, for the animals are capable of sex change. The largest and strongest is the male and the others are females.

Centropyge acanthops defends a territory fiercely, which means that fish added later will be chased off for two or three days. If you later add dwarf angelfishes that are too small, they will be killed, and you should not add any fish with similar coloration to the African Orange-backed Pygmy Angelfish; *Centropyge loriculus* is an example.

Centropyge acanthops is nonetheless a worthwhile pet, even for the less-experienced aquarist.

CENTROPYGE BICOLOR (BLOCH, 1787)

Blue-and-Gold Pygmy Angelfish

Centropyge bicolor, a dwarf angelfish with a maximum length of about 6 inches, is a relatively uncommon resident of the entire equatorial realm of the central and western Pacific Ocean. The fish is found in pairs or small groups on the steep slopes of reefs where coral growth flourishes.

To date, knowledge about what the fish eat in their natural habitat is incomplete. In the literature, information on this subject is sketchy or not given at all. This may mean that what we are looking at is a feeding specialist. This state of affairs might explain why many *Centropyge bicolor* do not last long in an aquarium—even in a reef aquarium—although they do accept food.

The Blue-and-Gold Pygmy Angelfish, usually imported from the Philippines, should be added to a tank only as very young specimens. It is possible that at such an early age specialized feeding on certain invertebrates has not progressed to the point that the fish's body depends on them. This is the fish's only chance to have a long life in an aquarium.

Centropyge bicolor is one of the problem species. It is best left for the more experienced marine aquarist. Photo by K.H. Choo.

The most difficult phase in the care of *Centropyge bicolor*, and one that must be gotten through, is the period of acclimatization—the first six weeks after the fish has been put into the aquarium. The difficulty is not necessarily just feeding, for many animals take to the substitute diet—*Mysis, Artemia*, and, especially, chironomid larvae—right from the start. The real problem lies in the assimilation of the food. You must also confront the unexpected—sudden refusal to eat, for example.

Although the Blue-and-Gold Pygmy Angelfish is certainly not one of those species that absolutely refuses to eat, it is advisable to offer greens continuously in the form of various algal preparations. In fact, algae is indispensable as a food for this species and sometimes also the impetus for its starting to eat other food once again.

In addition to feeding difficulties, susceptibility to disease is highly increased. Here, however, you can do something: keep a 30-watt UV light on 24 hours a day.

In spite of all your efforts, the fish may still die in about a year. If you keep it in a reef aquarium, a longer life may be possible, especially if species of stony corals with large polyps are among the inhabitants. Observation has shown that stony corals of the genus *Favia* are especially well suited to provide *Centropyge bicolor* with an acceptable substitute diet. This may be the fish's preferred food in the wild.

Any aquarium setup in which this fish feels at home will have as many hiding places as possible. Furthermore, it is advisable to choose as tankmates a group of peaceful fishes and, above all, none that are greedy eaters. Here, too, the reef aquarium is a good choice; the problem with different kinds of stony corals has already been mentioned.

Several individuals should be kept, the eventual harem being placed in the tank all at once following the proven formula: several different-sized fish at the same time. Chances for success will be best if all the animals in the group are eating, for feeding competition plays an important role.

In conclusion, this species certainly can only be recommended for the most experienced marine aquarists.

SUMMARY

Centropyge bicolor is one of those dwarf angelfishes whose care in an aquarium must be listed as problematic.

The best success is achieved in a reef aquarium. Make sure that the Blue-and-Gold Pygmy Angelfish has plenty of large-polyp stony corals and species of the genus *Favia*, the brain corals, around. There is a possibility that these stony corals are the natural foods of this fish in the wild.

This dwarf angelfish should be kept in groups along with other peaceful aquarium companions, because the company of other, more adaptable fishes and feeding competition make the transition to aquarium type feeding much easier. In addition to the obligatory frozen and flake foods, it is essential to give them algae. This species is only for the experienced aquarist.

CENTROPYGE EIBLI KLAUSEWITZ, 1963

Eibl's Pygmy Angelfish; Jeweled Angelfish

Eibl's Pygmy Angelfish is one of those dwarf angelfishes that have become known only recently. The German scientist Ireneus Eibl-Eibesfeldt discovered the fish in 1963 on the reefs of the Maldive Islands. The fish was named in his honor.

Presently, the known range of *Centropyge eibli* has been expanded to include Sri Lanka, Indonesia, and North West Cape of Western Australia. In its

A Coral Beauty (*Centropyge bispinosus*) displaying before a Keyhole Pygmy Angelfish (*C. tibicen*) on the Great Barrier Reef. This may be a territorial dispute. Photo by Walter Deas.

natural habitat—lushly populated reefs—Eibl's Pygmy Angelfish can be found at depths between 32 and 65 feet.

I have as yet no precise information about the food this species eats. According to Frank de Graaf, however, *Centropyge eibli* is very closely related to *Centropyge bispinosus*, so we can conclude that the diet is at least composed of the same elements: algae and small organisms of any kind.

No particular difficulties arise, then, when you keep *Centropyge eibli* in an aquarium. Given

plenty of *Caulerpa* and lots of hiding places, Eibl's Pygmy Angelfish will be a pleasure to watch as it eagerly goes for whatever kind of food you offer it.

Little is known about the mating behavior of this fish, either. Again, we must turn to *Centropyge bispinosus* and look for parallels. In so doing, we see that keeping this species in small groups of three to five individuals is just as advantageous as for most other dwarf angelfishes. Do not get old animals, and keep what you get in a reef aquarium. Sex-related differences in coloration are not known, but here, too, sex change may be a factor in pair formation. Thus, within a short time, your group should have a male and a hierarchy of females.

Interesting, but not particularly unusual in marine environments, is the color mimicry of the juvenile stage of *Acanthurus pyroferus*, the Chameleon Surgeonfish (Kittlitz, 1834). Juveniles of the acanthurid look like young *Centropyge eibli*. The similarity in the coloration of the two species is so confusing that inexperienced marine aquarists can easily mix them up. Before you get your *Centropyge eibli*, then, it is a good idea to take a look at the preopercle to see whether the spine typical of the angelfishes is present. Moreover, juveniles of *Acanthurus pyroferus* also mimic the basically yellow colored *Centropyge heraldi* and the gray and dark brown *Centropyge vroliki*.

Because *Centropyge eibli* is generally easy to care for, this fish makes an interesting pet even for beginners.

SUMMARY

Because it quickly adapts to a

substitute diet and is relatively hardy in fending off ectoparasites, *Centropyge eibli* is one of those dwarf angelfishes whose keeping quality in an aquarium can be termed good. A fixed portion of the diet should consist of algae in keeping with the situation in the natural habitat. Like many dwarf angelfishes, *Centropyge eibli* needs lots of caves and niches to hide in if it is to do well.

The fish do best if kept in a group of three to five juveniles. Within the group, one male will develop and the rest will be females.

In general, there is no nibbling on sessile invertebrates, but with living animals there is never any guarantee. Each fish has to be considered as an individual and cannot be forced into a particular mold.

With a size of between 4.8 to 6 inches, Eibl's Pygmy Angelfish is among the smaller dwarf angelfishes.

CENTROPYGE FERRUGATUS RANDALL & BURGESS, 1972

Rusty Pygmy Angelfish

Centropyge ferrugatus, like *C. bispinosus* and *C. eibli*, is a frequent import from the Philippines. The fish fauna of the Philippine coasts is among the richest to be found in tropical marine waters.

The Rusty Pygmy Angelfish lives at depths between 40 and 100 feet and grows to 4 inches in length. The species inhabits coral biotopes from the southwest tip of Taiwan to Tanabe Bay, 270 miles from Tokyo. It is also found in the vicinity of

Okinawa and the Ryukyu Islands. There the mostly solitary species feeds on algae and all kinds of small organisms.

Centropyge ferrugatus, less attractively colored than some of the other angelfishes, is quite easy to care for in an aquarium. It accepts a substitute diet quickly. It also picks continuously at algae and catches small crustaceans living between rocks and algae. The aquarium should be richly furnished, just as for all dwarf angelfishes.

Sometimes there are slight color differences among individuals of *Centropyge ferrugatus*, which lead some aquarists to the conclusion that the fish shows phenotypic sex differences. However, no proof for this supposition has yet appeared; the color differences may have their origin in regional differences.

Unlike what I have advocated for the previously covered species, this one is best kept in twos—each a different size. It is important to put them into the aquarium at the same time. Here, too, reef aquaria are better than simple fish aquaria, all the moreso since to date there have been no observations of damage to invertebrates by this species. *Centropyge ferrugatus* is a fish whose coloration is less gaudy than others, but one that can be recommended for beginners.

SUMMARY

Centropyge ferrugatus is a species that, in most cases, proves to be a worthwhile, durable member of an aquarium community. Like all dwarf angelfishes, this one should be kept in a reef aquarium because it is much easier to care for in that environment and its behavior is more natural. Beyond that, attacks on invertebrates have not yet been observed.

This fish will swiftly catch any delicious bit floating in the water, whether it be *Mysis*, *Artemia*, or any other frozen food, and even

A large reef tank may house several different species of pygmy angelfish. Three species can be seen in this photo. Photo by R. Wederich.

Eibl's Pygmy Angelfish (*Centropyge eibli*) inhabits lushly populated reefs. It is hardy and may be considered even for beginners. Photo by Roger Steene.

flake food. It is best to keep two animals of different size. Do not try to establish a harem in any aquarium holding less than 260 gallons.

CENTROPYGE LORICULUS (GÜNTHER, 1860)

Flame Pygmy Angelfish; Fiery Angelfish

One of the most beautiful and rarest of all the dwarf angelfishes is *Centropyge loriculus*. The Flame Pygmy Angelfish is native to waters around the tropical islands of the central and western Pacific, including the Hawaiian islands, Marshall Islands, and Johnston Atoll, to name a few. There, the natural habitat of *Centropyge loriculus* begins at a depth of about 20 feet.

This fish, about 2.8 inches in length, forms harems typical of dwarf angelfishes and lives in crevices, caves, and other hidden places.

Centropyge loriculus is one of the easiest of its genus to keep, which, along with its coloration, makes it one of the most attrac-

A juvenile *Centropyge eibli* in a dealer's tank. Photo by Joachim Frische.

tive inhabitants of an aquarium. The sight of a group of four or more of these mostly bright red fish swimming around in a reef aquarium looking for food is unforgettable.

Although, during the acclimatization phase the fish eat crustaceans and plant material taken from the aquarium furnishings, their interest will soon switch to live, swimming brine shrimp. Frozen chironomid larvae also catch their attention and are invariably gobbled up. Later on, not even flake and tablet food will be ignored, and, in fact, they enrich the fish's diet considerably. Unfortunately, *Centropyge loriculus* also like to dine on the large polyps of stony corals, xeniids, and the mantles of killer

An adult *Centropyge eibli* (about 12 cm total length) at Christmas Island in the Indian Ocean. Photo by Dr. G. R. Allen.

clams (*Tridacna*). They will nibble on these ceaselessly, and eventually the affected invertebrates will no longer open properly.

Spawning behavior, particularly in reef aquaria, has already been noted frequently, and there is hope that soon we will have news of young being reared from the fertilized eggs. For years, it was thought almost impossible to raise *Amphiprion* species, but nowadays it is a relatively simple undertaking. This gives us reason for optimism for other areas as well, such as the successful rearing of marine angelfishes.

Although *Centropyge loriculus* is a hardy fish, I recommend it only to the experienced aquarist.

SUMMARY

Centropyge loriculus is one of the most durable and beautiful representatives of its genus. Care is not excessively difficult, especially if you provide lots of hiding places and a varied diet,

Centropyge ferrugatus is best kept in a reef tank in twos—each a different size!. Photo by Joachim Frische.

beginning with plant material and including small organisms that live in the aquarium, the obligatory frozen foods, and even flake and tablet foods.

This hardy little dwarf angelfish, kept in groups, is almost made for life in aquaria. It should be kept in a reef aquarium that does not contain large-polyp stony corals, xeniids, and *Tridacna*, for these invertebrates may fall victim to the Flame Pygmy Angelfish. Because of its limited range, this fish should be reserved for extremely experienced aquarists.

CENTROPYGE POTTERI (JORDAN & METZ, 1912)

Potter's Pygmy Angelfish

Here I present another species from the genus *Centropyge* that arrives on our markets through Los Angeles: *Centropyge potteri*. It is endemic to the Hawaiian Islands. The species is quite common in its natural habitat, pebbly, rocky, coral bottoms at depths of about 40 feet.

Potter's Pygmy Angelfish, which grows to a maximum of 4 inches, is quite easy to care for in an aquarium. It quickly takes to the foods you offer, such as various kinds of insect larvae, *Mysis*, *Artemia*, and small krill. In addition to the frozen foods, the various commercial dried foods are also accepted. In the wild, the basis of its diet is algae and small crustaceans. In aquarium care, algae and lots of hiding places are essential if your goal is to keep Potter's Pygmy Angelfish properly.

Once again, the aquaria we call reef aquaria—those containing a number of sessile invertebrates combined with a few fishes—are ideal. One disadvantage of a reef aquarium is that it awakens the curiosity of *Centropyge potteri*, which likes to nibble on anything that

The bright red *Centropyge loriculus* is called the Flame Pygmy Angelfish or Fiery Angelfish for good reason. Photo by Dr. John E. Randall.

Centropyge loriculus can be kept in groups in a reef aquarium (without large-polyp stony corals, xeniids, or *Tridacna*). It also forms harems. Photo by James H. O'Neill.

Centropyge loriculus **lives in caves, crevices, or other hidden places in the reef. Photographed at Nauru by Dr. Dwayne Reed.**

even looks like food. As a rule, invertebrates are only bothered for a short time, but it may also happen that a particular sessile invertebrate—a killer clam of the species *Tridacna gigas*, for example, turns out to be particularly delicious. Then you have to decide between the fish and the invertebrate. This is not inevitable, however; there are many examples of *Centropyge potteri* being kept with various species of *Tridacna* without any problem at all. Once again, it is a matter of individual character, and it is almost a waste of time to try to formulate a rule.

We recommend keeping this fish in groups according to the proven principle of several different-size animals put into the aquarium at the same time, even though observations in nature and in aquaria do not provide precise information on the matter.

Spawning behavior of Potter's Pygmy Angelfish is like that of all dwarf angelfishes, as a study by Phil S. Lobel (1987) has shown. As the light fades in the evening, the male begins his courtship; he flares his fins and dances circles around the female. As courtship proceeds, both animals move into the open, where the male begins to nudge the female's belly. At the climax of courtship, the two fish shoot up to one of the uppermost points of their territory and release eggs and sperm simultaneously into the water. As water currents mix the gametes, the dwarf angelfish pair disappears into the protective cover of the reef.

SUMMARY

Centropyge potteri is one of those dwarf angelfishes whose care is quite problem-free, especially in an aquarium housing many sessile invertebrates—a reef aquarium. Unfortunately, some invertebrates, primarily species of killer clams, may be damaged. Any food, whether just thawed, still frozen, or in tablet or flake form, is eagerly taken.

If you want to keep your pet for years, you have to give it plenty of hiding places and a good growth of algae. Try to keep animals of this species in groups,

Centropyge potteri, an Hawaiian endemic, is easy to care for, especially if kept in a reef aquarium. Photo by Dr. G. R. Allen.

even though the observational reports have not yet provided any information on the subject.

CENTROPYGE TIBICEN (CUVIER, 1831)

Keyhole Pygmy Angelfish

Centropyge tibicen, which grows to 7.2 inches in length, is probably the largest of the dwarf angelfishes. It is found throughout the Indo-Australian Archipelago and around Taiwan and Japan as well. Its simple coloration, a black body with different shapes to its white spot on its side, has earned it its second name: Bright-spot Dwarf Angelfish.

The Keyhole Pygmy Angelfish is one of the more active of the dwarf angelfishes. It chases every aquarium inhabitant it feels big enough to take on, showing no respect even for large angelfishes.

Among the first food items that it takes are chironomid larvae. These bits of food drifting along in the current awaken great interest in the fish and form the major portion of its diet during the period of acclimatization. To obtain the bulk required for a smooth digestion, *Centropyge tibicen* always eats great quantities of algae, too. It may be a while before the menu of *Centropyge tibicen* includes *Mysis*, *Artemia*, krill, and various insect larvae.

The dark coloration of this fish makes it easy to spot the white, pinhead-size spots indicative of ich and *Oodinium*; this is important for beginners because we know that the most effective way to treat ectoparasites is to catch them early.

A young Keyhole Pygmy Angelfish, *Centropyge tibicen*. Its name is derived from the white lateral spot that resembles a keyhole. Photo by Kok-Hang Choo.

To keep the lively Keyhole Pygmy Angelfish happy, the aquarium should have plenty of decorations and places for the fish to hide briefly, on the spur of the moment. *Centropyge tibicen* will visit the open spaces of the

An adult Keyhole Pygmy Angelfish. This species can also be recommended for beginners. Photo by Earl Kennedy.

aquarium only rarely, and then only when its search for food takes it there. The reason for this timidity is to be found in its black coloration, which makes it highly visible to predators when it is out in the open.

If one of its tankmates appears hostile to the Keyhole Pygmy Angelfish, the front half of its body turns gray-brown as threatening behavior. The angelfish will spread all of its fins, just as it would during courtship. It shows the same coloration when it is courting a female or seeking the attention of a cleaner wrasse (*Labroides dimidiatus*).

However, the gray-brown color also appears if the fish is in ill health and, if it remains that way for a while, it is an important indication that the keeper should show some concern about its condition. For

example, the pH value may be too low, the animal may be suffering from constipation, or an attack of ectoparasites may be beginning.

For the rest, *Centropyge tibicen* is a fish that can be kept as well in a fish aquarium as in a reef setup, although the second one is preferable because it is more like the natural habitat.

We also recommend a group situation for this dwarf angelfish; it offers the keeper interesting insights into its social behavior.

SUMMARY

Centropyge tibicen is one dwarf angelfish that can be recommended for beginners. During the acclimatization phase the fish eats vegetable material and substitute food as well. Any initial feeding difficulties can be overcome by offering chironomid larvae.

One thing that makes this fish easy for beginners to keep is the ready recognition of an attack of ectoparasites; the first of the white spots are easy to see against the black of the fish's body. This early detection virtually guarantees successful treatment in almost every instance.

You can recognize different moods through a color change, from black to gray-brown. But if this coloration remains for a while, you should suspect that the fish is not in good health. You have to find out the reason for the color change in order to deal with it effectively.

In *Centropyge tibicen* you have an active fish, one that needs an abundance of places to hide, because it avoids open spaces.

This fish is good for either fish or reef aquaria, although the latter is preferable because of its resemblance to the natural habitat. No attacks on invertebrates have yet been described. Here, too, it is advisable to keep the fish in groups, although its size does not make this a simple matter.

GENUS: *GENICANTHUS*

In outward appearance, fishes of the genus of the lyretail angelfishes do not look much like angelfishes. From a distance they look more like fairy basslets than angelfishes. Only close observation of the preopercle turns up the typical spine that characterizes the angelfishes.

Not only is the anatomy of species of the genus *Genicanthus* quite unusual, its behavior also differs considerably from that of the other genera of the family Pomacanthidae. In its natural habitat, which, in the wild, is

This differential coloration led, at first, to the sexes being described as separate species. But, thanks to modern diving techniques, observations of the lyretail angelfishes have cleared up this mistake.

So far, not much is known about sex changes in the genus *Genicanthus*. The main reason is that the fishes live in such deep water that it is relatively seldom imported.

For the same reason, we know little about the care of lyretail angelfishes, so we advise caution

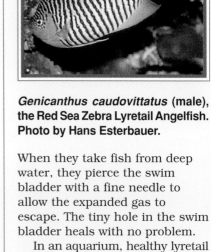

Genicanthus caudovittatus (male), the Red Sea Zebra Lyretail Angelfish. Photo by Hans Esterbauer.

When they take fish from deep water, they pierce the swim bladder with a fine needle to allow the expanded gas to escape. The tiny hole in the swim bladder heals with no problem.

In an aquarium, healthy lyretail angelfishes must be kept in small groups consisting of one male and two or three females. These fishes are ideal subjects for a reef aquarium because they do not damage invertebrates and will live for a long time only in such an environment. As a rule, fish aquaria do not offer an environment that allows lyretail angelfishes to develop to their fullest.

The best situation for fishes of this genus is a well-established aquarium at least 4 feet long, for these fishes are active swimmers. There have to be plenty of hiding

Genicanthus bellus (female), the Magnificent Lyretail Angelfish. Photo by Dr. D. Terver, Nancy Aquarium.

found in deep water on the steep sides of reef troughs, species of *Genicanthus* are found in groups, both large and small. In contrast to the rest of the angelfishes, lyretail angelfishes like the open water and avoid the bottom. In open water, they feed on drifting plankton.

In addition to looking and acting unlike other angelfishes, males and females of the genus *Genicanthus* show typical color differences (sexual dichromatism).

in buying one. If the fish do not swim normally but rather seesaw in an uncontrolled manner, there is probably a defect in the swim bladder. The condition is most likely due to the fish's having had insufficient time for decompression when brought up from its deep water habitat; consequently, the swim bladder expanded out of control and finally burst. Such animals are destined to die. Many fishermen take measures to avoid this.

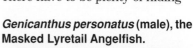

Genicanthus personatus (male), the Masked Lyretail Angelfish.

places, too, because when danger threatens the animals take cover in an instant. Just as important, however, is adequate room for swimming. In short, you have to be somewhat creative when you keep these fishes.

Give small-size food such as newly hatched brine shrimp nauplii, frozen foods such as *Daphnia*, fish and lobster eggs, *Cyclops*, and Bosminids. Later, they will also enjoy adult brine shrimp and small *Mysis*. These lyretail angelfishes catch their food in open water. Once the food is lying on the bottom, it ceases to be interesting.

Genicanthus personatus (female), the Masked Lyretail Angelfish. Photo by Scott Johnson.

Genicanthus watanabei (female). Photo by Dr. Fujio Yasuda.

Genicanthus watanabei (male). Photo by Dr. Fujio Yasuda.

A juvenile female *Genicanthus lamarck*, with the upper body stripe connected with the lower caudal band. Photo by Dr. Herbert R. Axelrod

Intermediate stage between male and female *Genicanthus semifasciatus*.

Tankmates for species of *Genicanthus* should be peaceful fishes that are not heavy feeders and do not defend territories vigorously.

Genicanthus currently includes about nine species:

Genicanthus bellus Randall, 1975 = Magnificent Lyretail Angelfish

Genicanthus caudovittatus (Günther, 1860) = Red Sea Zebra Lyretail Angelfish

Genicanthus lamarck (Lacepède, 1802) = Lamarck's Lyretail Angelfish

Genicanthus melanospilus (Bleeker, 1857)= Zebra Lyretail Angelfish

Genicanthus personatus

Randall, 1975 = Masked Lyretail Angelfish

Genicanthus semicinctus (Waite, 1900) = Half-striped Lyretail Angelfish

Genicanthus semifasciatus (Kamohara, 1934) = Half-banded Japanese Lyretail Angelfish

Genicanthus spinus Randall, 1975 = Pitcairn Lyretail Angelfish

Genicanthus watanabei (Yasuda & Tominaga, 1970) = Watanabe's Lyretail Angelfish

Although there is little information to be found about the general behavior of many lyretail angelfishes, courtship and spawning behavior in a few species has been documented in detail.

Lyretail angelfishes are capable of sex change. Females can become males whenever a group loses its male. Changing back again to a female, however, has not yet been documented. Although the change itself can happen quickly, it is several weeks before the new male assumes its typical coloration.

On the other hand, not much has been written about the spawning behavior of species of *Genicanthus*. The only known fact is that all species of the genus are free-spawners, which has been documented photographically several times.

At the time of expulsion, lyretail angelfish eggs measure about 750-800 micrometers, or 0.03-0.032 in. Newly hatched larvae, usually about 0.06 inch long, are quite small, and their feeding habits have not yet been documented even though investigations have been carried out in the natural habitat and in aquaria as well.

The genus *Genicanthus* is one of those groups of marine angelfishes that are very well suited for aquarium care. They are peaceful fishes and, in general, have no feeding problems in captivity.

Because of their size, which in nature seldom exceeds 8 inches, and the color differences between the sexes, care in a reef aquarium

offers an additional advantage, leading to hopes that soon more reports based on experience will be published than has been the case until now.

GENICANTHUS LAMARCK (LACEPEDE, 1802)

Lamarck's Lyretail Angelfish

The Lamarck's Lyretail Angelfish inhabits the steep sides of reef trenches off the Moluccas and New Guinea. Less frequently, it is found off the New Hebrides and Solomon Islands. Most specimens, however, are shipped from the Philippine Islands. Adult specimens may reach a length of about 9.6 inches, making *Genicanthus lamarck* the largest lyretail angelfish known to date.

should be kept in a reef aquarium, because only here will they develop and flourish properly. In addition, *Genicanthus lamarck*, like its relatives, is excellent for keeping with invertebrates, for it leaves them absolutely alone. Give this lively but timid fish plenty of hiding places, so it can take shelter immediately if danger threatens.

In general, Lamarck's Lyretail Angelfish is quick to adapt to substitute food as long as it is small enough. It enjoys chironomid larvae and *Artemia*, but also will not refuse Bosminids and water fleas. Further down the line it will also take freeze-dried and dried food. This makes Lamarck's Lyretail Angelfish very easy to keep.

An adult female *Genicanthus lamarck*, with the body stripes reduced almost to lines. Photo by Dr. Fujio Yasuda.

Male animals can be distinguished from females by the pale yellow spot on the forehead. Furthermore, males are distinguished by their longer tail fins.

If you are thinking of getting Lamarck's Lyretail Angelfish, make sure at the shop that the fish is swimming normally, and not wriggling seemingly uncontrollably with its head down. That is a sure sign of a defect in the swim bladder.

For aquarium life, it is essential that you keep several of these animals; the aquarium should be a minimum of 4 feet long. It goes without saying that the fish

You should know, however, that fishes that are too lively and are heavy feeders should not share an aquarium with *Genicanthus lamarck*; the latter might come up short at feeding time. In Japan, efforts to get *Genicanthus lamarck* and *Genicanthus semifasciatus* to spawn have been successful. Unfortunately, the article by Katsumi Suzuki is written in Japanese, so I cannot give any information about aquarium conditions here other than the highlights that were given in the English abstract: After a period of development lasting 20 hours, the larvae hatch and are about 0.06 inch long. After another 12 hours, they measure 0.08 inch. Sixty hours later, the eyes have formed, the mouth and anus have opened, and the yolk sack is used up. At this point, about three days after hatching, the larvae measure about 0.12 inch. Now they begin to take food in the form of different kinds of plankton. However, young have not yet been successfully reared in the aquarium.

SUMMARY

An active swimmer, *Genicanthus lamarck* needs a long aquarium—at least 4 feet long. The aquarium should offer plenty of places to hide so that these timid fish can take shelter when necessary.

Natural behavior develops properly only when the fish are kept in a group consisting of at least one male and two to four females. You can recognize the male by his yellow forehead spot and longer tail fin.

Lamarck's Lyretail Angelfish, an easy-to-keep fish, needs a varied diet of bite-sized food such as small *Artemia* and chironomid larvae.

If possible, do not keep the Lamarck's Lyretail Angelfish with other reef-type aquarium fishes that are too lively. This species does not bother invertebrates.

GENICANTHUS WATANABEI (YASUDA & TOMINAGA, 1970)

Watanabe's Lyretail Angelfish

Although *Genicanthus watanabei* was discovered only recently, it is astonishing to see that the species is relatively common in the trade. Its natural range extends from Taiwan to southern Japan and northern Okinawa. Specimens have also been seen on Osprey Reef, off the northern coast of Queensland, and in the vicinity of Lanford Island.

In its natural habitat, Watanabe's Lyretail Angelfish grows to a maximum length of 6 inches. The species can be found on steep slopes at depths of between 200 and 230 feet. Animals from such depths require correct decompression if they are to reach the surface of the water uninjured.

Aquarium care is usually without complications, but here, too, a reef aquarium is preferable. The fish also need a long tank, at least 4 feet long, an abundance of hiding places, and peaceful tankmates. As with all lyretail angelfishes, a group of the usual composition is preferred because it is consistent with behavior and habits.

The sexes of Watanabe's Lyretail Angelfish differ consider-

Male *Genicanthus watanabei*. Photo by Roger Steene.

ably with regard to color. If the aquarist does not know this, he will hardly recognize that they belong to the same species. Females of *Genicanthus watanabei* are silvery white with a small, blue-bordered eye stripe and a shimmering bluish forehead spot. In addition, the anal and dorsal fins have blackish blue borders. Males have, on the lower flanks, black stripes against a silvery white background. In addition, there is a horizontal yellow stripe in front of the tail fin.

If you give it bite-size food, feeding is no problem; the diet can consist of any of the known kinds of food.

SUMMARY

In a long aquarium with plenty of hiding places and peaceful tankmates, a small group of *Genicanthus watanabei* consisting of one male and two to four females will do extremely well.

Once again, I cite reef aquaria as the best environment for this fish, because their invertebrate inhabitants help simulate natural conditions and, as a rule, guarantee better water conditions than a fish aquarium. This species is suitable for a community tank because it does not grow too large and does not bother the invertebrates.

Feed it with bite-size bits of frozen, dried, and freeze-dried food.

Males and females differ so greatly in coloration that it is easy to mistake them for two different species.

A pair of *Genicanthus watanabei* (male right, female left).

GENUS: *CHAETODONTOPLUS*

THE VELVET ANGELFISHES

I shall treat the genus *Chaetodontoplus* as a unit, not mentioning individual species. The reason for this is that species of this genus appear only sporadically in the trade, and, furthermore, most of the species are not regarded as easy to care for. To date, the genus has nine species, listed as follows:

Chaetodontoplus ballinae Whitley, 1959 = Balina Velvet Angelfish; Pearl-gray Velvet Angelfish

Chaetodontoplus chrysocephalus (Bleeker, 1854)= Yellow-headed Velvet Angelfish

Chaetodontoplus conspicillatus (Waite, 1900) = Spectacled Velvet Angelfish; Collared Velvet Angelfish

Chaetodontoplus cyanopunctatus Yasuda & Tominaga, 1976 = Blue-spangled Velvet Angelfish; Crystal Velvet Angelfish

Chaetodontoplus duboulayi (Günther, 1867)= Duboulay's Velvet Angelfish

Chaetodontoplus melanosoma (Bleeker, 1853)= Black Velvet Angelfish; Phantom Velvet Angelfish

Chaetodontoplus mesoleucus (Bloch, 1787) = Vermiculated Velvet Angelfish; Smoky Dwarf Velvet Angelfish

Chaetodontoplus personifer (McCulloch, 1914) = Bluemask Velvet Angelfish

Chaetodontoplus septentrionalis (Temminck & Schlegel, 1844) = Blue-lined Velvet Angelfish

From a distance, the genus *Chaetodontoplus* closely resembles the butterflyfishes, family Chaetodontidae, which is probably the reason why this genus of marine angelfishes was named *Chaetodontoplus*. In spite of some anatomical similarities to butterflyfishes, the genus

Chaetodontoplus chrysocephalus, the Yellow-headed Velvet Angelfish. Photo by Dr. Fujio Yasuda.

Close-up of the head of *Chaetodontoplus conspicillatus*. Photo by M.P. & C. Piednoir.

Chaetodontoplus conspicillatus, the Spectacled Velvet Angelfish. Photo by Roger Lubbock.

Young *Chaetodontoplus melanosoma* (25mm SL). Photo by Dr. Fujio Yasuda.

Head shot of a *Chaetodontoplus meredithi*. Photo by Walter Deas.

Adult *Chaetodontoplus melanosoma*. Photo by Gerhard Marcuse.

Adult *Chaetodontoplus meredithi*. Photo by Roger Steene.

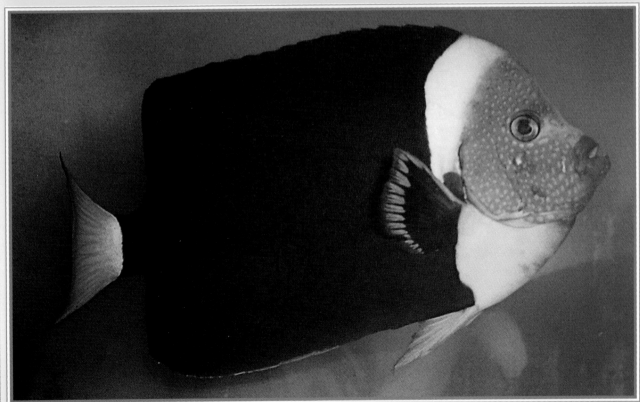

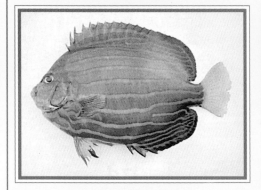

Above: *Chaetodontoplus septentrionalis* adult. Photo by Dr. Shih-chieh Shen.

Right: *Chaetodontoplus mesoleucus.* Photo by Dr. Gerald R. Allen.

Below: *Chaetodontoplus duboulayi.* Photo by Dr. Herbert R. Axelrod.

Chaetodontoplus duboulayi. Photo by John O'Malley.

Chaetodontoplus melanosoma. Photo by Joachim Frische.

Chaetodontoplus caeruleopunctatus. Photo by Joachim Frische.

Chaetodontoplus meredithi. Photo by John O'Malley.

Chaetodontoplus is a true angelfish, as the preopercular spine clearly shows.

Velvet angelfishes, as they are commonly called, are native to waters from Japan to Australia, with two species in the Pacific Ocean from the Solomon Islands to New Caledonia. The maximum size, attained in a few species, is around 10 inches. As a rule, however, most of the species are fully grown at about 8 inches.

Aquarium care for these species is little known or written about. True, there are reports on the care of individual animals, but such articles are the exception. Species of *Chaetodontoplus* require large aquaria, from 80 to 100 gallons or more. In addition, they need a number of hiding places in the form of caves and crevices, a good growth of algae, and peaceful, slow-feeding tankmates. Although these angelfishes are usually not aggressive toward others, this may not be the case with fishes of similar coloration or other members of the genus *Chaetodontoplus*. It is nonetheless always a good idea to keep at least 3 animals of the same species of this genus so that there will be fewer problems with feeding and acclimatization. Make sure to put different-sized animals of the same species in at the same time. Here, too, the smaller the better, because adult fish almost never learn to feed properly.

The reef aquarium is certainly a sensible alternative to a purely fish aquarium, but you cannot rule out attacks on the invertebrates, at least by the larger species. Reports of experiences with smaller species of *Chaetodontoplus*, such as *Chaetodontoplus mesoleucus*, indicate that keeping them with invertebrates presents no problems.

Fishes of this genus take to a substitute diet only with reluctance, and when they do it is a diet of *Mysis*, *Artemia*, and

Chaetodontoplus conspicillatus in a reef tank. Photo courtesy of Midori Shobo.

Chaetodontoplus septentrionalis (young). Photo by Dr. Fujio Yasuda.

Chaetodontoplus septentrionalis (subadult). Photo by Kok-Hang Choo.

chironomid larvae, and sometimes also krill and dried food. Feeding with clams has proven highly successful. Living bivalves, such as *Cardium* or *Mytilus*, are opened and placed in the aquarium as is. Of course, in addition to animal food, do not forget to include vegetable matter.

Chaetodontoplus duboulayi is an exception to the rule with regard to aquarium care. It adjusts quite easily to aquarium life, even in a purely fish aquarium. It is also an exception to other members of its genus with regard to sex differences. Males have a bright white spot behind the eyes. In females, the white spot is faint. Given this phenotypic difference, it is easy to make up a pair.

Little is known about courtship and reproductive behavior in *Chaetodontoplus duboulayi*, because the fish is relatively uncommon within its range off the coast of Australia.

Published information about egg development is available only for *Chaetodontoplus septentrionalis*. The articles come from the pen of the Japanese Shiro Fujita. Larvae of *Chaetodontoplus septentrionalis* hatch after about 20 to 24 hours. According to this information, water temperature should be between 80 and 82.5 degrees F. Forty-eight hours after hatching, the larvae usually measure 0.1 inch and the yolk sack is completely consumed. Eyes, mouth, and anus have developed, and nothing stands in the way of beginning to feed on plankton.

We hope that the future will bring more experience with species of this genus, whether observations in the natural habitat or in aquaria.

SUMMARY

With regard to the aquarium care of individual species, we can state that there are problems, at least with feeding. However, two species, *Chaetodontoplus duboulayi* and *C. septentrionalis*, seem to be exceptions.

This genus should be reserved only for marine aquarium experts who have aquaria full of algae, or, better yet, who have reef aquaria and are aware of the risk that, under certain circumstances, one or another of the invertebrates may end up as dinner.

There is no problem keeping these fishes with others, although a community including other species of velvet angelfishes may present problems. If two individuals of the same species are kept together, a good idea in many respects, it is important that they be added at the same time.

GENUS: *APOLEMICHTHYS* FRASER-BRUNNER, 1933

Apolemichthys arcuatus is called the Hawaiian Pearlyscale Angelfish. It is endemic to the Hawaiian Islands. Photo by Dr. Herbert R. Axelrod.

Armitage's Angelfish, *Apolemichthys armitagei*, comes from the Western Indian Ocean. Photo by Aaron Norman.

In this chapter I present the fourth genus of the family Pomacanthidae, *Apolemichthys*, but I will describe in detail only the one representative of the genus that is encountered quite frequently in the trade, *Apolemichthys trimaculatus*. The rules for the care of this fish generally apply to the other species of the genus as well. With a length of roughly 12 inches, *Apolemichthys trimaculatus* is the largest member of its genus, which presently consists of nine species, listed as follows:

Apolemichthys arcuatus (Gray, 1831) = Hawaiian Pearlyscale Angelfish

Apolemichthys armitagei Smith, 1955 = Armitage's Angelfish

Apolemichthys griffisi (Carlson & Taylor, 1981) = Griffis's Angelfish

Apolemichthys guezei (Randall & Mauge, 1978) = Reunion Angelfish

Apolemichthys kingi Heemstra, 1984 = Tiger Angelfish

Apolemichthys trimaculatus (Cuvier, 1831) = Three-spotted Angelfish; Blue-mouth Angelfish

Apolemichthys xanthopunctatus Burgess, 1973 = Gold-spangled Angelfish

Apolemichthys xanthotis Fraser-Brunner, 1951 = Red Sea Angelfish

Apolemichthys xanthurus Bennett, 1832 = Indian Smoky Angelfish

The genus *Apolemichthys* is one of those genera that has been described only in our century. This genus, along with *Pygoplites*, was first described in 1933 by Fraser-Brunner. Before that, species of both genera had been assigned to the genus *Holacanthus*.

All the fishes of this genus have one thing in common: aquarium care is not without its problems. As indicated above I will discuss only the one species.

APOLEMICHTHYS TRIMACULATUS (CUVIER, 1831)

Three-spot Angelfish; Blue-mouth Angelfish

Apolemichthys trimaculatus has a broad Indo-Pacific distribution, being native to the reefs of the Philippines, the eastern part of the Indo-Australian Archipelago, the South African coast, and Mauritius and the Seychelles. Its natural food is primarily sponges, algae, and crustaceans.

I frequently see Three-spot Angelfish about 4 inches long on the market. At this size, the fish have achieved their final coloration. In any event, the color change from juvenile to adult is not as pronounced as in other genera of marine angelfishes.

Juveniles differ from adults in that they lack the black-and-white banded anal fin. Instead, it is entirely yellow. The bands appear when the fish is between 1.6 and 2.4 inches long. Furthermore, juveniles of *Apolemichthys trimaculatus* have a black eyespot in the soft-rayed portion of the dorsal fin that disappears when the fish is about 3 inches long.

For aquarium care, it is best to get individuals measuring 3 to 4 inches in length. One prerequisite for the care of *Apolemichthys trimaculatus* is stable water conditions. In addition, a lush growth of algae is essential for their well-being, and plenty of natural hiding places must be provided through abundant decorations.

Keeping this fish in a reef aquarium requires some thought, for attacks on invertebrates are unavoidable. But, as is so often reported, marine angelfishes that are considered difficult adjust better in this kind of aquarium. If there is an attack on one of the invertebrates, give some thought

Apolemichthys trimaculatus is one of the most common species of the genus. It has a broad Indo-Pacific distribution. Photo by Dr. Herbert R. Axelrod.

With *Apolemichthys trimaculatus*, it is best to purchase individuals about 3-4 inches in length. Photo by John O'Malley.

Apolemichthys xanthotis will turn up only in shipments from the Red Sea as it is a Red Sea endemic. Photo by Guy van den Bossche.

The Gold-spangled Angelfish, *Apolemichthys xanthopunctatus*, occasionally appears in the pet trade. Photo by Dr. John E. Randall.

to not keeping that one in the future. Alternatively, you can no longer keep *Apolemichthys* in your reef tank. Proper care in a fish aquarium with plenty of algal growth may also be rewarded with success.

The first feeding is usually plant material. After a while, the usual kinds of frozen foods follow, with *Artemia* and chironomid larvae the favorites. It takes a while, however, before the fish begin accepting a substitute diet. Once *Apolemichthys trimaculatus* is acclimatized, however, individuals may even be tempted to accept flake and tablet food. As already mentioned, the period of acclimatization is problematic, although some aquarists report otherwise.

One result of being caught, shipped, and held under less than optimal conditions is that *Apolemichthys trimaculatus* is susceptible to skin infections and skin parasites. With regard to ectoparasites, what *Paracanthurus hepatus* is to surgeonfishes, *Apolemichthys trimaculatus* is to marine angelfishes. More than any other fishes, these two species react to sudden changes in environment or gradual deterioration of water quality by developing an attack of ectoparasites, recognizable by white spots. In the primarily blue *Paracanthurus hepatus* the disease is quickly and easily detected, but the yellow coloration of the Three-spot Angelfish makes the task more difficult, putting experience to the test. I have already discussed the treatment of ectoparasites elsewhere in this book.

With regard to keeping this species with others, I can report that it is peaceful at least with tankmates of different coloration. It is only possible to put two animals of the same species together if the animals are not the same size and are put into the aquarium at the same time. It is just about impossible to add one later.

In addition to *Apolemichthys trimaculatus*, you sometimes also find *A. arcuatus* and *A. xanthurus* on the market.

SUMMARY

Apolemichthys should be reserved for experienced aquarists.

Specimens measuring between 3 and 4 inches are most likely to adapt to life behind glass. A prerequisite for long years of aquarium life is good, stable water values and conditions, which argues in favor of a reef aquarium. Unfortunately, attacks on invertebrates of various kinds cannot be excluded. In any event, there should be plenty of algae in the aquarium, as well as an abundance of places to hide.

The conditions described are also applicable for the other species of the genus *Apolemichthys*, as a few articles on the subject have stated.

There is no problem with keeping this fish with other fishes. The simultaneous placing of two individuals of a single species is, as a rule, successful; later addition of another specimen seldom turns out well. This fish should be kept in an aquarium holding a minimum of 75 to 100 gallons.

The Tiger Angelfish, *Apolemichthys kingi*, was fairly recently described and is not commonly seen by aquarists. It was named for Dennis King. Photo by Dennis R. King.

Another relatively recently described angelfish is this *Apolemichthys griffisi*. Photo by Aaron Norman.

GENUS: *HOLACANTHUS*

All species of this genus inhabit the tropical Atlantic and eastern Pacific Oceans. *Holacanthus venustus*, from the tropical western Pacific, is an exception. But this species has meanwhile been assigned to a new genus, *Sumireyakko*, which, to this date has only one known species.

In contrast to the species of the genus *Pomacanthus*, the mouth of species of the genus *Holacanthus* is shaped like a parrot's beak. They are as a rule sponge-feeders, and large animals are unsuitable for reef aquaria, for they can pick just about any invertebrate to pieces. But if you are ready to limit yourself to those invertebrates that it does not eat, you will have an aquarium of a very special kind.

Common to most all species of the genus *Holacanthus* are long dorsal and/or anal fins; sometimes the upper tip of the tail fin is also extended. In species of *Pomacanthus* and related genera this latter feature is usually found only in *Arusetta asfur*, *Pomacanthus arcuatus*, *Pomacanthus maculosus*, *Pomacanthus paru*, and *Pomacanthus semicirculatus*.

As in *Pomacanthus* species, all juveniles change colors as they mature. The differences in coloration between the developmental stages, however, are not as pronounced as in their relatives.

The species of the genus *Holacanthus* are extremely territorial; in nature they form false harems. The section on "Sex-related Characters, Pair Formation, and Mating Behavior" at the end of this book contains more information on the various forms of harems described.

Without a doubt, among the most popular representatives of this genus is *Holacanthus ciliaris*.

Angelfishes grow to a considerable size and must be kept in a correspondingly large aquarium, one that holds at least 200 gallons. With good care, which

A *Holacanthus passer* in its juvenile coloration. Photo by John O'Malley.

naturally includes good water quality, all species of *Holacanthus* quickly become tame and will eat from their keepers' hands.

If you have decided to keep species of *Holacanthus*, it is essential to remember to get small animals. Larger ones measuring more than 4 inches in length frequently have problems during the acclimatization phase. This is expressed through susceptibility to ectoparasites and refusal to eat.

Happily for us, breeding stations—large outdoor aquaria that open into the sea—have been established recently in the U.S., some of which are rearing species of the genus *Holacanthus*.

An aquarium set up for species of *Holacanthus* should offer not only an abundance of places to hide but plenty of swimming room as well. It is a good idea, then, to choose a very long tank.

Essential for the well-being of every species of *Holacanthus* is regular consumption of plant material. In addition to algae, spinach and lettuce are good. Whether offered in bite-size pieces or fastened whole to a rock, this food is eagerly accepted. Make sure that any plant matter that does not grow in the aquarium itself is first cooked.

Be especially careful with these angelfishes when they are undergoing their color change, an extremely difficult and stressful phase for them. A change in water conditions or rearrangement of decorations can bring on an attack of ectoparasites. In addition, the fish may suddenly refuse food or even die unexpectedly from heart failure, if they are not equal to the demands.

The best thing to do when acquiring an angelfish is, as already described, to get a small one in its juvenile coloration. Such an animal will bring you the greatest pleasure, for you can watch it grow, and it will long be one of your favorite companions. Adults or almost fully grown individuals usually last only a short time in an aquarium, especially since it is difficult to determine the fish's age. Most important, however, is that you will miss the satisfaction of having raised the angelfish yourself.

species presented, *Holacanthus townsendi*. *Holacanthus townsendi* is not really a separate species in the true sense because it cannot reproduce. It is, rather, a sterile hybrid, the result of crossing *Holacanthus bermudensis* with *Holacanthus ciliaris*. The Queen and Blue Angelfishes are found in the tropical Western Atlantic Ocean,

A juvenile *Holacanthus ciliaris*. Photo by John O'Malley.

where both may grow to 18 inches. Their basic food is sponges.

When buying either of the two species, make sure to get juveniles not more than 4 inches long. Larger animals may present problems, particularly during the acclimatization phase.

It is not easy to tell the difference between the juveniles of the two species—it takes a practiced eye. In contrast to *Holacanthus ciliaris*, *H. bermudensis* is a lighter yellow; *H. ciliaris* is more of an orange color. Furthermore, the striping shows slight differences as it crosses the body. In *H. bermudensis*, the stripes are

Holacanthus townsendi is a hybrid between H. ciliaris and H. bermudensis. Photo by Dr. Walter A. Starck II.

HOLACANTHUS BERMUDENSIS
GOODE, 1876
Blue Angelfish; Bermuda Angelfish

HOLACANTHUS CILIARIS
(LINNAEUS, 1758)
Queen Angelfish

HOLACANTHUS TOWNSENDI
The species *Holacanthus bermudensis* (with *Holacanthus isabelita* as a synonym) and *Holacanthus ciliaris* are treated together here, for they are cared for in almost exactly the same way. They are very closely related, as can be suspected from their coloration, which, apart from the blue forehead spot that *Holacanthus ciliaris* has and *Holacanthus bermudensis* lacks, is quite similar. And, finally, from these two fishes comes the third

An adult *Holacanthus ciliaris*. It is recognizable by the solid yellow tail and "crown" of blue and black on the nape. Photo by John O'Malley.

whitish blue and mostly run in a straight line across the body. In *H. ciliaris*, the stripes are a deep blue and run in a slight curve. Because the coloration is so similar, you have to know a trick to keep the two in the same aquarium. You have to put them in at the same time. If you put them in at different times, at an interval of a week or two, the older one will harass the newcomer and, under certain circumstances, kill it.

Although differentiating between the two juveniles is not always easy, there is no problem in this regard with adults. Unlike *Holacanthus bermudensis*, *H. ciliaris* has a black forehead spot rimmed in blue; the black spot is itself covered with little blue spots.

Keeping the different kinds of *Holacanthus* species together is no problem either. The keeping of Queen and Blue Angelfishes, however, requires some knowledge in their care and handling. Although juveniles take easily to a substitute diet, they make high demands on water quality. Even a slight change in one of the water parameters can lead to the appearance of a powdery, sugar-like growth on the skin, which is not necessarily easy to notice because of the yellow color of the body. Once the animals have become emaciated, there is not much you can

do to help them. You may also observe that the fish avoids touching the decorations with its opercula—an indication that gill worms are present.

The aquarium should be set up with a large choice of hiding places. At first, these are frequently used. Because *Holacanthus* species are always territorial, this behavior continues in the aquarium and sometimes leads to harassment of and attacks on other tankmates.

It is astonishing to see how quickly *Holacanthus ciliaris* and *H. bermudensis* develop trust for their keeper. After just a short time, they accept tablet and flake food or the obligatory frozen food, from his hand, which never ceases to be an indescribable feeling.

Juvenile Blue and Queen Angelfishes can be cared for in a reef aquarium without special preparation, although there should be no crustose anemones or sponges in it. Then there will not be any complaints about attacks on invertebrates. With increasing age, however, this peaceful behavior can turn to curiosity about the forbidden food, and this can make care in a reef aquarium impossible. Alternatively, limit yourself to those invertebrates that neither species will touch; among these are leather corals of all genera,

disk anemones, tube corals, and, of course, any invertebrate that can move out of the way, such as shrimp, sea urchins, and starfishes.

SUMMARY

Holacanthus ciliaris and *H. bermudensis* should be reserved for the hand of the expert. At a size of less than 4 inches, they do not present as many problems as larger animals. In general, they are sensitive to changes in water conditions, usually reacting by breaking out in a parasitic skin infection—not easy to recognize on the body of a yellow fish. Lack of appetite usually goes hand in hand with an attack of ecto-parasites, and this may cause the fish to become emaciated quickly.

Aquaria for both species should be set up with plenty of niches, caves, and crevices, which the animals enjoy visiting. A green carpet of algae and a mass of the higher algae are not out of place and serve as between-meal food for the fishes. They can also be fed both dried and frozen food.

Keeping both species in the same tank is problematic because their coloration is so similar; it will be successful only if they are introduced at the same time when they are both juveniles. Although young animals are easy to take care of in a reef aquarium, as long as there are no crustose anemones in it, this situation may unfortunately change as the fish get older.

Both the Queen and the Blue Angelfishes are very territorial, and this may lead to harassment of and even attacks on other species of fishes.

Once adjusted to life in the aquarium, both species are a feast for the eyes—pets that will give joy to their keeper for decades and, through their trusting natures, become integral members of the family.

An adult *Holacanthus bermudensis*. **This species has a yellow-edged tail and no "crown." Photo by Dr. Herbert R. Axelrod.**

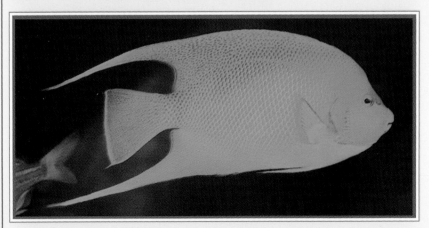

HOLACANTHUS PASSER VALENCIENNES, 1846

Passer Angelfish; Mexican Emperor; California Angelfish; King Angelfish

Holacanthus passer makes its home in the reefs along the tropical western coasts of the Americas as far north as the Gulf of California. There, the Passer Angelfish or Mexican Emperor lives in rocky areas in very clear water. Because of its distribution, *H. passer* is one of those angelfishes that should be kept in cooler aquaria. Temperatures around 72 degrees F are acceptable for good care. There is no problem, however, with temperatures between 79 and 82.4 degrees F, but in some situations, the angelfish's life expectancy may be sharply reduced.

In its natural habitat, the Passer Angelfish, which grows to 10 inches, feeds on tunicates, sponges, and other benthic invertebrates.

Holacanthus passer is one of the most durable fish known to the marine aquarium hobby. Juveniles are not sensitive to ectoparasites, take food without hesitation, and present no other problems for their keepers. Unfortunately, however, as these fish get older they become more aggressive. Their behavior may become so unbearable for other inhabitants of the tank that, if not hardy enough to withstand these assaults, they die. Any fish that is chased around only now and then is getting off lightly. But harassment may be prolonged and lead to attack from one minute to another without any recognizable reason. One minute the fish might be swimming side by side and the next minute *Holacanthus passer* is chasing the other one as though it had never seen it in the aquarium before. And it does not matter how large or how dangerous the opponent is. You get the impression that the Passer Angel would attack any inhabitant of the tank that entered its territory—and woe to the one that cannot stand up to *Holacanthus passer*.

Surprisingly enough, *Holacanthus passer* usually does not bother or eat invertebrates other than those that make up its natural diet, which makes it a good fish for a reef aquarium. It will also do well,

the sexes. Males of *Holacanthus passer* have snow-white pelvic fins, whereas those of the female are bordered in yellow.

If you are thinking of keeping *Holacanthus passer*, you should think it over carefully. If you decide to go ahead, having considered all the consequences of keeping an animal of this species, you will find yourself with a long-lasting, rewarding pet.

Holacanthus passer can be recommended to everybody. When obtained as a juvenile it presents no problems with regard to its care. Photo by Günter Spies.

however, in a fish aquarium holding at least 100 gallons.

Like all angelfishes, the Mexican Emperor needs plenty of places to hide, so that it can withdraw whenever it wants to.

You can only keep two *Holacanthus passer* together if you put them in at the same time and either both are juveniles or one is a juvenile and one an adult. For two fish, your aquarium absolutely must hold at least 200 gallons.

There is another possibility, however, that may be used for older animals, one based on the phenotypic differences between

SUMMARY

Holacanthus passer is one angelfish that can be recommended to every aquarist who has a taste for hardy fishes such as triggerfishes, surgeonfishes, and lionfishes. But it is also possible to keep it in a reef aquarium as long as you avoid keeping the animals that make up its natural diet.

Acquired as a juvenile, this fish presents no problems with regard to care. It is resistent to ectoparasites, usually eats whatever you offer it, and is otherwise without problems.

In addition to being large enough, the aquarium should

contain the decorations usually included for marine angelfishes, including algae. If there is no algae, cooked lettuce and spinach are an excellent alternative.

The main thing to remember in caring for this fish is that the water temperature should be consistent with what _Holacanthus passer_ is used to in its natural habitat—about 72 degrees F. It is possible to keep it at higher temperatures, but the fish's life expectancy is reduced.

HOLACANTHUS TRICOLOR (BLOCH, 1795)

Rock Beauty; Tricolored Angelfish

Holacanthus tricolor, which grows to a maximum length of 12 inches, lives in the tropical western Atlantic and in the Caribbean Sea. There, it is most likely to be found in caves, niches, and coral formations. Its

A subadult _Holacanthus passer_. This species usually will not bother the invertebrates of a reef aquarium. Photo by John O'Malley.

natural diet includes sponges, algae, zoanthids (crustose anemones), tunicates, and small crustaceans.

Although the juvenile stage of _Holacanthus tricolor_ is entirely yellow, aside from the blue-bordered spot toward the rear of its body, adult animals are brown on the rear two-thirds of their body. Only the head and fins still show the brilliant yellow of their juvenile coloration. As it matures, the Rock Beauty (one of the many common names for this species) undergoes a color change that causes it to resemble the demoiselle _Stegastes planifrons_. Only the preopercular spine and the somewhat high-backed body shape of _Holacanthus tricolor_ can clear up the confusion.

A reef aquarium is the ideal environment for the Rock Beauty, commonly found on the market at lengths of between 1 and 2 inches. There, the fish will nibble on anything that looks like food. Invertebrates are its natural food—especially crustose anemones, which you should avoid. But the Rock Beauty also enjoys commercial frozen chironomid larvae, and _Mysis_ and _Artemia_ as well. Just make sure that the food is bite-size. Dried food in its many variations is also a welcome supplement.

Unfortunately, it may happen that with increasing age the Rock Beauty becomes more interested in other sessile invertebrates. It may not eat them up entirely, but damage caused by nibbling is common. Gorgonians, in particu-

The Rock Beauty, _Holacanthus tricolor_, should be kept in a reef environment even though over the long run it may bother some of the invertebrate inhabitants. Photo by John O'Malley.

Juvenile *Holacanthus tricolor* have a different shape as well as a different color pattern than adults. Photo by Charles Arneson.

lar, may be affected. If worse comes to worst, you must either limit yourself to those invertebrates that are not bothered or decide to keep *Holacanthus tricolor* in another kind of aquarium.

There is no problem keeping small Rock Beauties with other aquarium inhabitants, even other marine angelfishes—on one condition. Do not include fishes that are greedy eaters, for eventually young *Holacanthus tricolor* will come up short at feeding time.

The territorial behavior of this fish, which usually entails increased aggression as it ages, should be noted here. The result is that fishes of similar coloration will be attacked, and harassment of adult *Holacanthus tricolor* is extreme.

It has been known for a while that *Holacanthus tricolor* is capable of sex change; this means that pair formation involving one large and one small fish is successful. Success is practically guaranteed if the fish are introduced simultaneously into a sufficiently large aquarium, one holding more than 150 gallons.

Only recently, I have learned that the sexes are colored differently, but this is noticeable only in sexually mature adults. Males have some pale reddish spots on the tail fin; these are lacking in the female. It takes a practiced eye, however, to identify the male as such.

In conclusion, I should say that *Holacanthus tricolor*, acquired as a juvenile, can be thoroughly recommended for beginners as long as they have a reef aquarium available. Otherwise, the animals may starve.

SUMMARY

If *Holacanthus tricolor* is acquired at a length of less than 4 inches, it will develop beautifully if fed a varied diet and kept in a tank with plenty of hiding places, good water quality, and lots of various kinds of algae.

During the first months of care, any tankmates should be peaceful ones, which means that a reef aquarium is the best choice. However, long-term care in a reef aquarium can bring problems because the fish, in accordance with its nature, often bothers one or another of the invertebrates. Gorgonians and crustose anemones are the prime victims.

If you put two different-size animals into the tank at the same time, after a while you will have a pair, for *Holacanthus tricolor* can change sex. You should take advantage of this characteristic and not keep the animals singly.

POMACANTHUS, EUXIPHIPOPS, AND ARUSETTA

Probably the best-known representatives of the marine angelfishes are those species that belong to the genus *Pomacanthus*, with *Pomacanthus imperator*, the Emperor Angelfish, undoubtedly the most famous of them all.

Presently, the genus *Pomacanthus* comprises eight species, the genus *Euxiphipops* three species, and *Arusetta* one species. Typical of all of them is a low-positioned mouth. When the animal is feeding, the lower jaw projects forward. In their natural habitat, these species feed primarily on sponges, algae, and crustaceans. All of these species have in common that they live reclusively among coral heads or near caves. Only seldom are they seen in open water.

All these species are territorial. The male has a large territory within which females defend smaller territories. The maximum length of species of *Pomacanthus* varies between 10 inches (*Pomacanthus chrysurus*) and about 20 inches (*Pomacanthus arcuatus*). In the aquarium, however, they do not grow this large.

In all of the species there is a surprisingly big difference between juvenile and adult coloration. The difference is so pronounced that for a long time juveniles were regarded as separate species. For example, juveniles of *Pomacanthus imperator* were given the scientific name *Pomacanthus nicobariensis*; while adults always had their present name, *P. imperator*. The latter name is now, of course, applicable to both developmental stages.

Most juveniles show a blue background color with variously arranged white stripes. Exceptions are *Pomacanthus arcuatus, P.*

paru, and *P. zonipectus*. These juveniles have various arrangements of yellow stripes against a black background. Why these three species developed different juvenile colorations in the course of evolution seems to be unknown.

The difference in coloration between juveniles and adults may be attributed to an extremely aggressive defense of territories against members of the same species. If little *Pomacanthus* about 0.8 inch long were already wearing adult colors, they would have no chance for survival. They would either be harassed to death by the adults or would leave the protective environment of decorations or natural structures and be eaten by predators. So this is how juveniles survive in adult territories, for the adults do not recognize any fish of a different color as being members of their own species. Just when the color change takes place in the natural habitat has not yet been investigated.

Good water conditions are a prerequisite for the care of these fishes. If a single animal is kept in an aquarium, color change begins when the individual is about 4 inches long. In nature, however, this may happen earlier; sometimes animals about 3 inches long come on the market that are already showing adult colors.

Marine aquarists can take advantage of the peaceful relations between juveniles and adults. The chapter on pair formation, sex-related characters, and mating behavior will treat this in more detail.

If possible, care of one of these angelfishes in an aquarium should begin in the juvenile stage. It is not always a simple matter, however, to tell what species you

have, for many juvenile angelfishes in this group differ from one another in coloration only slightly. Although a precise identification is not always possible, you should still try to get a juvenile of the species you want, for young of the genus *Pomacanthus* adapt quite easily to aquarium life. The process may be much more difficult for adult animals. Refusal to eat a substitute diet is a common, almost insurmountable problem with adult *Pomacanthus*, for by that time feeding specialization has become too well established.

In addition, for proper keeping of an adult *Pomacanthus*, you must have an aquarium that holds a minimum of 250 gallons, whereas juveniles will be satisfied with one holding about 130 gallons. If, however, adults do begin to eat and the aquarium is the right size, it still does not mean that all will be successful, for many adult *Pomacanthus* die during their first year of aquarium life, often without any discernible reason.

You should also be aware that when you buy a large *Pomacanthus*, it means that a pair back on the reef has been broken up, thereby endangering the preservation of the species. In these days of environmental awareness, acquisition of young animals is the only reasonable way to counter the objections of those opposed to the saltwater aquarium trade.

The most difficult phase in the care of a young angelfish begins with the color change to the adult form. During this time, which in aquaria may be a year or two, the fish are very susceptible to disturbances, excessive stress, and fear. Even the addition of new fishes or the transfer to another aquarium may prove fatal. The reason may lie in the enormous expenditure of energy such a color change requires, for the fish become weak and react sensitively to external influences.

As mentioned at the beginning of this discourse, species of *Pomacanthus* eat, among other things, primarily sponges. But if a fish is kept in an aquarium with invertebrates, they should be only those that will not be disturbed, such as leather corals, disk anemones, stoloniferous anemones, and mobile invertebrates such as sea urchins and shrimp. It is not advisable to keep them with clams, crustose anemones, and soft corals. But here, too, with increasing age the fish may attack even the invertebrates just mentioned as being safe.

Euxiphipops is described separately here because its care is different in some respects from species of *Pomacanthus*. Three species are included in this genus.

Euxiphipops navarchus and *E. xanthometapon* are known to every aquarist for their brilliant colors, but *E. sextriatus* is the little gray mouse of the genus. For this reason it seldom appears on the market. In addition, with its length of a good 20 inches, it is the largest of the three species.

All three species are delicate, and thus reserved for experienced aquarists; this is not the case for juveniles of *Pomacanthus*.

Another difference between this genus and *Pomacanthus* is the size at which *Euxiphipops* juveniles take on adult coloration. You will not find juvenile coloration in any fish larger than between 1.5 and 2.5 inches, which means that in pet stores, the fish offered for sale are almost exclusively adults. Why the juveniles take on adult coloration when they are so small is not known.

Care of the different species of *Euxiphipops* is difficult because they are especially demanding with regard to water quality. But the way the aquarium is set up

and the choice of tankmates are also critical for successful care. And I must mention the difficulty in taking food, especially for *E. navarchus*, because the problem is nearly insoluble for any aquarist. There is some chance for success in a reef aquarium, although many of the invertebrates will end up on the menu. Even leather corals and disk anemones are not rejected, either, and this diminishes the joy some aquarists might otherwise find in this species. Think it over carefully before realizing your wish to have pets belonging to one of these species.

EUXIPHIPOPS NAVARCHUS (CUVIER, 1831)

Blue-girdled Angelfish; Dream Emperorfish

Euxiphipops navarchus, commonly known as the Blue-girdled Angelfish, is certainly among the most beautifully colored, aggressive, and delicate of the large marine angelfishes. There is hardly another species to which the description just given would apply.

In nature, this fish, which grows to 10 inches in length, inhabits coral growths and the sloping sides of reefs at depths between 10 and 100 feet. *Euxiphipops navarchus* is also found in protected lagoons. The main source of imports is from the Philippines. In the trade, by far the greatest percentage of fish are in their adult coloration, because the blue and white coloration of the juveniles turns to that characteristic of adults when the fish is still quite small.

Care of *Euxiphipops navarchus* may entail an extremely difficult period of acclimatization, for the

A juvenile *Euxiphipops navarchus*. The Blue-girdled Angelfish is one of the most delicate of the large marine angelfishes. Photo by Earl Kennedy.

fish stubbornly refuses to eat. As a rule, if the Blue-girdled Angelfish is larger than 4 inches, all efforts to get it to eat any kind of food, including its natural foods such as sponges or crustose anemones, fail, and *Euxiphipops navarchus* starves to death.

It is a lucky aquarist whose fish begins to eat after about two weeks, usually taking food that is unfamiliar to it such as flake and tablet food. Tablets attached to the side of the tank are the most successful. And tablets are the food it takes if, after six to nine months, the Blue-girdled Angelfish begins to eat again without any discernible reason. This description applies to *Euxiphipops navarchus* more than 4 inches long.

The situation is different for small Blue-girdled Angelfishes. Here, the acceptance of a substitute diet is not the main problem—rather, it is death due to shock, for example, if a water change is performed too quickly.

In addition to these difficult circumstances, the problem of ectoparasites arises. The fish is susceptible to them and at the same time does not tolerate high dosages of medication, especially copper sulfate.

If the fish manages to accustom itself to some extent to aquarium life, it develops a higher-than-average level of aggression toward

Artificial sea salts are widely available in a number of different formulations. Photo courtesy Coralife/Energy Savers.

tankmates, especially newcomers.

Small Blue-girdled Angelfish are quite reclusive, but larger specimens are active continuously in the aquarium. Accordingly, there must be plenty of decorations and room for swimming as well. In addition, the often-cited algae are irreplaceable for this species in supplying bulk to the diet.

It is possible to keep *Euxiphipops navarchus* in a reef aquarium, especially if the specimens are small. But attacks on crustose anemones, sponges, soft corals, and clams are seldom reported for larger specimens, either. *E. navarchus* is most certainly only for extremely experienced marine aquarists.

SUMMARY

The Blue-girdled Angelfish, *Euxiphipops navarchus*, belongs in the hands of extremely experienced aquarists

who have large aquaria holding more than 180 gallons.

Blue-girdled Angelfish less than 4 inches long do not usually last very long, because they stubbornly refuse to eat. With small fish, unfamiliar food promises the greatest success; tablet food attached to the wall of the tank offers the best chances.

Unfortunately, small specimens of *Euxiphipops navarchus* are extremely sensitive to external influences such as a too-rapid water change, so you have to make certain that any work you do in the aquarium is done slowly.

Things that have a positive effect on care are a rich availability of algae, places to hide, and room to swim. Care in a reef aquarium is entirely possible and even recommended as long as it contains no invertebrates that will be eaten, such as soft corals and crustose anemones.

EUXIPHIPOPS XANTHOMETAPON (BLEEKER, 1853)

Yellow-faced Angelfish; Diadem Emperor

The second species of the genus *Euxiphipops* to be described here is the Yellow-faced Angelfish, *Euxiphipops xanthometapon*, which, in coloration and temperament, is quite comparable to *E. navarchus*.

This species is usually found on the market in its adult form, for here, too, juvenile coloration turns to adult coloration at a very early age. The Yellow-faced Angelfish, which grows to 20 inches in the wild, adapts most easily to aquarium life when it is between 2.4 and 4 inches long.

The main exportation of *Euxiphipops xanthometapon* is also from the Philippines, although some specimens come from Singapore and Indonesia. The most beautifully colored ones,

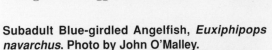

Subadult Blue-girdled Angelfish, *Euxiphipops navarchus*. Photo by John O'Malley.

however, are surely those that come from the Maldives.

Yellow-faced Angelfish live among coral formations and the slopes of reefs at depths of between 10 and 100 feet. There, the species feeds primarily on sponges and algae.

If the fish make it into your aquarium in good condition, they will spend the first few days hiding among the protective decorations. Very gradually, they leave the safety of their hiding places and slowly begin to explore the new surroundings. As a rule, the first food is plant material, so it is a good idea to have it available right in the aquarium in the form of different kinds of algae. In addition, the fish will enjoy eating the small crustaceans that live in the aquarium among the algae before beginning to try out the rich assortment of frozen and dried food you offer them. Once adapted to the tank, the Yellow-faced Angelfish is a very durable pet and does not present by far the difficulties of its cousin, *Euxiphipops navarchus.*

As in almost all pomacanthids, juvenile coloration is blue and white, making it no problem to keep young and adult animals together in a large aquarium, one holding 200 gallons or more. Here, too, the simultaneous introduction of two different-size adults is usually successful, with neither of them longer than 4 inches.

This fish should not be kept in a reef aquarium, for the species goes after soft corals, crustose anemones, sponges, and clams, and even disk anemones, gorgonians, and leather corals, sometimes destroying them completely. Unfortunately, it also happens that as it ages, the fish becomes extremely quarrelsome toward its tankmates, although this is not its usual behavior.

In conclusion, this fish cannot be unconditionally recommended for beginners; it is better for aquarists who already have some experience in the realm of keeping coral fishes.

A nearly adult Yellow-faced Angelfish, *Euxiphipops xanthometapon.* This species should only be kept in large aquaria of more than 200 gallons. Photo by John O'Malley.

SUMMARY

About the Yellow-faced Angelfish, I can say that animals between 2.4 and 4 inches long adapt to aquarium life without much difficulty. The aquarium should hold a minimum of 208 gallons and have lots of decorations and a good growth of various kinds of algae for the fish to feed on until it is ready to accept a substitute diet.

Euxiphipops xanthometapon is suitable for a reef aquarium under only very limited conditions, for it will at least try out almost any kind of invertebrate.

Sometimes, aggression toward tankmates can be severe, but here the Yellow-faced Angelfish is an exception to its kind.

Care of *Euxiphipops xanthometapon* can be recommended for any saltwater aquarist who already has accumulated some experience with other coral fishes.

ARUSETTA ASFUR (FORSSKAL, 1775)

Arabian Angelfish; Half-moon Angelfish

Arusetta asfur, also sometimes called *Pomacanthus asfur,* is endemic to the Red Sea and the Gulf of Aden. There, at depths between 10 and 49 feet, this extremely shy fish lives in cracks in rocks and caves in the protected inner parts of reefs. Although endemic, the species is relatively common there, primarily singly or in pairs.

Aquarium care for this species is considered to be problem free as long as the animals are less than 4 inches long when acquired. You can get juveniles just 2 inches long that already have their full adult coloration, with the beautifully shaped yellow moon that extends across the body as the fish ages.

Pomacanthus maculosus has similar coloration, with a similar yellow spot; the shape of the spot, however, varies from individual to individual. Furthermore, *P. maculosus* is more of a light blue, whereas *A. asfur* is a blackish blue. It is more difficult to tell the juveniles apart. They are an almost identical blue with white stripes; the only difference is in the tail fin—in *Pomacanthus maculosus* it is white and in *A. asfur* it is yellow.

The Arabian Angelfish is a willing feeder and will soon be eating any kind of food you offer it in tablet or flake form. Its main preference, however, is for any kind of frozen food, such as *Mysis, Artemia*, krill, chironomid larvae, and clam and fish flesh. To supplement the diet, of course, greenery in the form of algae, spinach, or lettuce should be offered. It goes without saying that, in keeping with the natural habitat, the aquarium should provide an abundance of hiding places; otherwise, this rather shy fish cannot develop fully.

When feeding angelfish, it is important to remember their full range of nutritional needs. Photo courtesy of Ocean Nutrition.

Arusetta asfur **is endemic to the Red Sea. It can be kept in a reef aquarium without crustose anemones, clams, or xenids in it. Photo by Gerhard Marcuse.**

Care in a reef aquarium is problem free as long as there are no crustose anemones, clams, or species of the family Xeniidae. To date, there have been no reports of attacks on other invertebrates. But this robust fish is also suitable for fish aquaria, for it certainly knows how to hold its own.

Recommended for their care is an aquarium with a volume of at least 180 gallons, for tanks that are too small will increase the natural aggression of this species. Unfortunately, aggression in *Arusetta asfur*, a territorial animal, should not be underestimated; it will go after any fish newly added to the tank. Fishes of similar coloration will be harassed to death. But fatal attacks have also been reported on fishes marked with vertical stripes, such as *Zanclus cornutus* or *Heniochus acuminatus*. Consequently, it is advisable to put these fishes into

the tank first and add *A. asfur* later, for observations have shown that this situation does not lead to attacks.

It is only possible to keep more than one *Arusetta asfur*, then, if the animals are put into the tank simultaneously, and one considerably smaller than the other, in either juvenile or adult coloration, or the two are different sexes, which is difficult to determine since there are no known phenotypic sexual characters. This angelfish would certainly be well suited for beginners if it were not for its aggressive personality.

SUMMARY

Arusetta asfur, which grows to about 12 inches, is endemic to the Red Sea, where it lives in crevices and caves of the inner part of the reef.

With regard to feeding and susceptibility to disease, aquarium care is problem free as long as the water quality is good and there are plenty of hiding places.

It is possible to keep *Arusetta asfur*, not more than 4 inches long, in a reef aquarium as long as there are no crustose anemones, clams, or xeniids in it.

Animals in juvenile coloration (blue with white stripes) must have a yellow tail fin; if it is white, the fish is a *Pomacanthus maculosus*.

Unfortunately, the fish is aggressive toward other fishes of similar coloration and fishes with white vertical stripes, but usually only if these fishes are placed in the tank later. Later placement of a second *Arusetta asfur* is possible only if the new fish is in its juvenile coloration or is much smaller than its counterpart.

Because of its aggressive behavior, beginners should stay away from this fish at first.

POMACANTHUS ANNULARIS (BLOCH, 1787)

Blue Ring Angelfish

The Blue Ring Angelfish belongs to that group of coral fishes that show again and again how views of aquarium care may differ. On the one hand, there is the opinion that the Blue Ring Angel is easy to care for; on the other, there is the view that *Pomacanthus annularis* should be regarded as a touchy pet. One thing is certain, however— *Pomacanthus annularis* belongs in the aquarium of an experienced caretaker.

In its native environment, the coral reefs of Sri Lanka, Indonesia, and New Guinea, *Pomacanthus annularis*, which grows to 12

especially since attacks on invertebrates are not observed. The first food taken is plant matter consisting of different kinds of algae growing in the aquarium. Later on, frozen and flake food placed in the tank will be eaten. Lettuce and spinach may also be substituted for algae. *Pomacanthus annularis* needs more plant food than many other marine angelfishes, and the foods just named are excellent supplements to the diet. Here, too, it is true that Blue Ring Angelfish less than 4 inches long adapt better to aquarium life than larger fish.

The adult color pattern is just starting to become visible in this young Blue Ring Angelfish, *Pomacanthus annularis*. Photo by John O'Malley.

inches in length, feeds mostly on sponges, primarily red species. In addition, its diet includes all kinds of crustaceans, bryozoans, and bristle worms.

Juveniles, which come primarily from Indonesia, are demanding in their care. They need abundant hiding places, algal growth, and good water conditions. Keeping juveniles in a reef aquarium is certainly appropriate,

Juvenile Blue Ring Angelfish less than 4 inches long that already have their adult coloration are certainly the most durable, for they have not yet developed the feeding specialization of their adult counterparts and they do not have to go through the strength-sapping coloration change.

Once *Pomacanthus annularis* finally begins to eat, it is a rewarding pet, one that will live for years in an aquarium (as long as it has a volume of at least 200 gallons). Given plenty of places to hide (the fish may stay hidden for hours at a time), this animal is quite peaceful, leaving tankmates alone as long as they are not the same color as itself. Although the correct choice of species, made right at the dealer's tanks, decides whether the marine aquarist is getting an easy or a difficult pet, this is still no fish for beginners.

SUMMARY

Pomacanthus annularis should be acquired at a size of less than 4 inches. It is even better if the fish is already showing its adult coloration, which means that the difficult color-change phase is over.

Under the conditions already described, adaptation to aquarium life presents few problems. Green matter is essential, especially since *Pomacanthus annularis* needs it more than many other marine angelfishes do. To supplement the diet, add frozen and flake food as well as lettuce and spinach.

These extremely shy fish require the presence of many hiding places to prevent their behavior from becoming abnormal; under certain circum-

Pomacanthus chrysurus (a subadult seen here) comes from the western Indian Ocean. It requires plenty of room, plenty of hiding places, and plenty of algae. Photo by John O'Malley.

Juvenile *Pomacanthus chrysurus* have the "typical" striped pattern of many species of *Pomacanthus*. Photo by John O'Malley.

stances, they might become aggressive toward tankmates.

Care in a reef aquarium has thus far been problem free, so this kind of environment is recommended for keeping the fish for a long time without difficulty. Care of this species should be reserved for experienced aquarists.

POMACANTHUS CHRYSURUS (CUVIER, 1831)

Yellow-tailed Angelfish

Pomacanthus chrysurus arrives regularly on the market from the coasts of Kenya. Most are juveniles in the blue-and-white coloration typical of many angelfishes, and this is a good thing because fully colored specimens frequently have problems with feeding.

Because juveniles of *Pomacanthus chrysurus* have, in

addition to the blue body color and white stripes, a yellow tail fin, care must be taken to insure that it is not confused with *A. asfur*, whose juveniles also have a yellow tail. It is characteristic of *P. chrysurus* that the yellow tail fin is divided by two intertwined white bands.

Pomacanthus chrysurus occurs not only off the coast of Kenya but in the northwestern parts of the Indian Ocean, off the Seychelles and the East African coast from the Gulf of Aden to Zanzibar. The natural biotope consists of everything from rocky coasts and dead reefs to lagoons with isolated coral growths and even intact coral reefs. Very little is known about the diet of this fish in the wild, but probably sponges, crustaceans, and algae are part of it.

The maximum length of the Yellow-tailed Angelfish is about 12 inches, which means that an aquarium holding at least 180 gallons is required. In an aquarium, the fish needs plenty of nooks and crannies, and plenty of algae is essential. In such a setup, juveniles of *Pomacanthus chrysurus* quickly accept a diet of *Mysis*, chironomid larvae, and *Artemia*. Later on, it will also usually accept dried and freeze-dried food.

There have been many reports of successful care of this species in reef aquaria when the animal did not exceed 2.4 to 3.2 inches. If the Yellow-tailed Angelfish is larger, the keeper has to keep his eye on invertebrates of the genera *Xenia*, *Cespitularia*, and *Anthelia*, for these will sometimes be attacked.

So far there is no hint of color-related sex differences, which means that two individuals of *Pomacanthus chrysurus* can only be kept together successfully if one juvenile and one adult are introduced into the tank at the same time, or if both fish are placed simultaneously in an aquarium that is new to them both. If you do not follow this

advice, it will happen, as with cichlids in fresh water, that the long-established *Pomacanthus chrysurus* will kill a new arrival of the same species and coloration. If you are introducing a new fish, take the old one out first.

Juveniles can be recommended for beginners, then, if the parameters of the aquarium water are good, there are plenty of hiding places, there is a lush growth of algae, and the other aquarium inhabitants are not too lively. The other alternative is to keep the fish in a reef aquarium,

If you want to keep several animals of this species, which is advisable, make sure to put all of the *Pomacanthus chrysurus* at once into a tank unfamiliar to them. This is a must if the animals you have acquired are all of the same coloration. The situation is different if you are adding a new fish of one coloration to a tank holding a well-established member of the same species but with different coloration.

Pomacanthus chrysurus is suitable for a reef aquarium if the fish you keep are smaller than 3.2

An adult Emperor Angelfish, *Pomacanthus imperator*, can grow to a length of more than a foot. On the reef its natural diet includes sponges and algae. Photo by John O'Malley.

for there are no problems in store for you there.

SUMMARY

Pomacanthus chrysurus adapts readily to aquarium life if it is acquired in its juvenile coloration.

The prerequisite for successful care is a large aquarium with a volume of at least 180 gallons, lots of decorations, and a good growth of algae. After a few days, the fish takes to a substitute diet readily; brine shrimp are an essential part of that diet.

inches when you get them, and if you do not keep invertebrates of the genera *Xenia*, *Anthelia*, and *Cespitularia*. If these points are observed, the Yellow-tailed Angelfish can be recommended for beginners.

POMACANTHUS IMPERATOR (BLOCH, 1787)

Emperor Angelfish; Nicobar Angelfish

In 1787, the ichthyologist Bloch saw *Pomacanthus imperator*, and from then on classified every

The juvenile Emperor Angelfish has a distinctive pattern of circles or almost-circles and is easily recognized. Photo by John O'Malley.

species that resembled *P. imperator* as members of the marine angelfish family. To date, this has not changed.

The Emperor Angelfish occurs on the reefs of the Red Sea, off the coast of South Africa, and as far as Hawaii and the northern part of the Great Barrier Reef of Australia. In parts of its range, for example in the Red Sea, as it ages, *Pomacanthus imperator* develops a little fan at the end of its soft-rayed dorsal fin. Why this character is regional has thus far not been explained. Also unclear is why Red Sea Emperor Angelfishes have a red tail fin instead of the usual yellow one.

On the reef, the Emperor Angelfish, which grows to 12 inches in length, feeds on sponges and algae.

Care in an aquarium holding at least 200 gallons is quite simple for juveniles of *Pomacanthus imperator*. The little Emperor Angelfish are always on the prowl for food, eating practically anything that looks edible.

Young Emperor Angelfish are, however, sensitive to poor water conditions. If the water conditions are really poor, the fish refuse to eat and consequently fall victim to attacks of ectoparasites. To do well, small specimens of the Emperor Angelfish need considerably more plant matter in their diet than their larger counterparts do. Although the care of young Emperors is relatively simple, that of larger fish in adult coloration is a real trick. After a year in the tank, adult *Pomacanthus imperator* may suddenly refuse to eat, without any particular reason. In addition, it is the larger fish in adult coloration that are really susceptible to parasitic attacks. Along with the parasites common to Emperor Angelfishes, atypical diseases may occur. For example, white specks 0.04-0.08 inches across on the skin may appear which, as the disease progresses, may resemble a snowy forest. Large Emperors are just as susceptible to poor water conditions. They react quickly with milky or bulging eyes; blindness has even been reported several times.

With regard to feeding, adult Emperor Angelfish are extremely choosy. They only accept particular kinds of frozen food, and frequently only for a short period of time. In the long run, adult Emperors will eat only mussels and sometimes also tablet food. Tablets are taken only when they have been previously broken into bite-size pieces, and the pieces are dropped, with the aid of a plastic tube, right in front of the fish's snout. Simply attaching the tablets to the side of the tank will not bring the desired results. If *Pomacanthus imperator* suddenly stops eating, it is not easy to get it to start again. The most successful strategy is to use the tablet method just described. It goes without saying that algae are a basic food for this fish and that they have to be available in sufficient quantity.

An aquarium set up for *Pomacanthus imperator* should offer an abundance of caves and niches, for, in its natural habitat on the reef, this species spends as much time in its shelter as it does in open water looking for food.

Be careful when putting Emperor Angelfish with other angelfishes. *Pomacanthus imperator* is extremely quarrelsome, a behavior you can see even in juveniles.

Keeping *Pomacanthus imperator* with sessile invertebrates becomes more problematic as the fish gets older; your stock should be limited to leather corals, disk anemones, and tube corals.

SUMMARY

Acquired in its juvenile coloration, the Emperor Angelfish is a durable pet, which, if fed a varied diet and with good water conditions, grows and thrives.

Plenty of algae is advantageous, but if there is none, spinach and lettuce will do.

Easy as it may be to take care of young *Pomacanthus imperator*, this is not a beginner's fish, and, in spite of everything, it should be kept only by experienced aquarists.

I do not advise keeping a *Pomacanthus imperator* larger than 4 inches. At that point the problems begin, whether it is sensitivity to deteriorating water parameters or difficulties with feeding. The larger the animal at the time of acquisition, the smaller its chances of living for a long time in the aquarium.

Aquarium decorations should provide an abundance of caves and crevices, for Emperor Angelfish spend the greater part of their day in such shelters, only seldom venturing out into the open water.

Keeping this fish with other angelfishes is not without problems, for *Pomacanthus imperator* is definitely territorial.

It is worth trying to keep invertebrates only with juvenile Emperor Angelfish. With increasing age, the species diversity of your invertebrates will shrink unavoidably.

POMACANTHUS MACULOSUS (FORSSKAL, 1775)

Blue Moon Angelfish

Like *Pomacanthus chrysurus*, *P. maculosus* comes from the coastal reefs of Kenya and is exported all over the world. Unlike *P. chrysurus*, however, *P. maculosus* is difficult to care for.

The prerequisite for successful care is acquisition of young Blue Moon Angelfish. Juvenile animals are also blue and have white vertical stripes. The tail fin, however, is white—an important criterion in identification of this species, which otherwise is easy to confuse with *Arusetta asfur*.

Pomacanthus maculosus and *A. asfur* resemble one another in their juvenile coloration, and adults are not always immediately distinguishable either. *P. maculosus* lacks the yellow tail fin that is found in both juvenile and adult stages of *A. asfur*. Moreover, the lateral marking of the Blue Moon Angelfish is more like a spot and shows considerable variation from one individual to another; it is certainly no sex-related character.

Pomacanthus maculosus, which grows to 12 inches, inhabits the tropical reefs of the

Arabian peninsula. Its range extends further to the northwestern part of the Indian Ocean, the entire Red Sea, and the Persian Gulf. In these regions, Blue Moon Angelfish generally live at depths between 13 and 39 feet in places where coral grows abundantly.

Like all large angelfishes, the natural diet consists of algae, sponges, and small crustaceans. At the size already mentioned, and in an aquarium holding a good 200 gallons, the fish will soon be enjoying the obligatory frozen food.

Care in a reef aquarium is successful if invertebrates of the genera *Xenia*, *Anthelia*, and *Cespitularia* are avoided. Crustose anemones of the genus *Zoanthus* may be eaten, too. Naturally, the aquarium has to have many hiding places and plenty of algal growth, for this species, like the others, requires plant matter for bulk if it is to digest its food optimally. Attacks on

A juvenile *Pomacanthus maculosus*. Care in a reef tank is usually successful as long as certain invertebrates are excluded. Photo by John O'Malley.

The juvenile French Angelfish, *Pomacanthus paru*. It is best to acquire this species as a juvenile because it acclimates to captivity better. Photo by John O'Malley.

A young adult *Pomacanthus paru* from the Caribbean is accepting the ministrations of a cleaner wrasse (*Labroides dimidiatus*) from the Indo-Pacific without hesitation. Photo by Joachim Frische.

the invertebrates mentioned above were mostly observed when plant food was either in short supply or the colonies were damaged in one way or another.

Pomacanthus maculosus is a peaceful member of its genus and is thoroughly suited for beginners as long as the prerequisites described are taken to heart.

SUMMARY

The Blue Moon Angelfish is one of those species of the genus *Pomacanthus* that adapt rapidly and without problems to aquarium life as long as they are acquired when they are between 1.5 and 2.5 inches long. They soon take and enjoy the different foods offered. Like all large marine angelfishes, if this one is to do well it needs a large aquarium with a healthy stand of algae and lots of hiding places.

Pomacanthus maculosus is a peaceful fish as long as no others of its species with the same coloration and of the same sex are introduced later into the aquarium. Blue Moon Angelfish in their juvenile coloration are suitable for a reef aquarium if you dispense with invertebrates of the family Xeniidae.

POMACANTHUS PARU (BLOCH, 1787)

French Angelfish

The French Angelfish arrives on the market usually as a juvenile. The juvenile coloration of *Pomacanthus paru* is different from that of the previously described species. Here, the ground color is black and the vertical stripes are yellow. The tail fin is bordered in yellow. Juveniles of *P. arcuatus* and *P. zonipectus* also show this coloration. The juvenile colors of the Gray Angelfish, *P. arcuatus*, and *P. paru* are strikingly similar, and the fish are often mistaken for one another. The two species can be distinguished best through the yellow-bordered tail fin of *P. paru*, which is lacking in *P. arcuatus*.

Reefs in the tropical Atlantic at depths of up to 200 feet are home to the French Angelfish. Based on investigations of stomach contents that have been conducted on some of the animals, we know that this species feeds primarily on sponges. Algae, too, are an essential constituent of the diet. In addition, a small portion of the diet consists of gorgonians, zoantharians, tunicates, spermatophytes, eggs, hydroids, and bryozoans. The composition of the natural diet leads to the conclusion that this species is basically unsuitable for being kept in a reef aquarium, for there even the leather corals, unknown in the tropical Atlantic, will sometimes be eaten. Even juveniles of *Pomacanthus paru* tend to regard xeniids, gorgonians, and soft corals as a tasty change from their normal diet, and will not turn up their noses at tridacnas, either.

It pays to acquire juveniles of this species because they present no difficulties during the acclimatization phase. In addition to the

Adult *Pomacanthus paru* on the reef. Photo by Günter Spies.

substitute food that you give them—in flake, tablet, or frozen form—there are also hardly ever problems with ectoparasitic attacks, as long as water conditions are correct and there is ample plant food. If the French Angelfish is in the midst of its color change, or if adults are acquired, aquarium care is considerably more difficult and not always successful.

Pomacanthus paru is one of those large marine angelfishes that can be contentious with other tankmates, especially with species that have vertical stripes, such as *Chelmon rostratus* or *Zanclus canescens*. Animals of the same species and coloration are vehemently attacked and sometimes harassed to death; size has nothing to do with this situation. Only animals that are introduced into the aquarium at the same time respect one another.

In conclusion, with its mature size of 20 inches, *Pomacanthus paru* is among the largest member of its genus and can thus be recommended only for aquaria holding more than 250 gallons of water. The fish is a good one for beginners.

SUMMARY

Juveniles of *Pomacanthus paru* adapt to aquarium life easily. They are soon eating the food you give them, especially enjoying tablet and flake food.

Of great importance for the well-being of this species is plant food in the form of algae, spinach, and lettuce. French Angelfish in transitional and adult coloration have difficulty adapting, and you should avoid acquiring such fish.

Unlike many juvenile angelfishes, these have a black ground color with yellow stripes; *Pomacanthus paru* and *P. arcuatus* look very much alike. The yellow border on its tail fin distinguishes *P. paru* from *P. arcuatus*.

With its mature size of about 20 inches, *Pomacanthus paru* belongs in an aquarium holding at least 250 gallons that also offers

Close-up of the face of *Pomacanthus semicirculatus*. Photo by Walter Deas.

an abundance of hiding places. This species is only good for a reef aquarium under certain conditions, for it nibbles on almost any kind of invertebrate. Juveniles of *P. paru* can be recommended even for beginners.

POMACANTHUS SEMICIRCULATUS (CUVIER, 1831)

Koran Angelfish

The Koran Angelfish is the most commonly imported marine angelfish. It occurs in almost all tropical areas of the vast Indo-Pacific region, which accounts for its ubiquitous presence on the market.

Its diet consists of sponges, algae, crustaceans, and small sea anemones. In nature, *Pomacanthus semicirculatus* grows to a length of 16 inches.

Koran Angelfish are often for sale as juveniles or in transition coloration; adults are seldom available. The reasons for this may be either that the adult coloration is less attractive or that the adult *Pomacanthus semicirculatus* is too aggressive. However that may be, juveniles are ideal for aquarium care.

The Koran Angelfish, *Pomacanthus semicirculatus*, is the most commonly imported large angelfish, but adults as large as this one are rarely, if ever, offered for sale. Photo by Pierre Laboute.

The juvenile Koran Angelfish. Photo by K. H. Choo.

After just a short time, the Koran Angelfish will be eating any conceivable kind of food with increasing appetite. From flake and tablet food to all kinds of frozen foods, to freeze dried food

and greenery—everything is accepted and eaten to the point that you must take care to see that the fish does not become incurably overweight in a very short time.

The Koran Angelfish can be kept even in water of barely good quality, but, of course, you should not aim for this low standard. Even susceptibility to skin, gill, and intestinal parasites is quite low. Just make sure that the reclusive lifestyle of this species is accommodated by providing caves and crevices for it to hide in.

Care in a reef aquarium is recommended for this species only under certain conditions, for as the fish grows it might well attack the most differing kinds of invertebrates.

Without a doubt, however, the beginner will find in this

fish an ideal partner, which should be kept in an aquarium holding at least 250 gallons to accommodate its size—up to 16 inches.

SUMMARY

The Koran Angelfish is one of those large angelfishes that can be recommended even to marine aquarists who have only a theoretical knowledge of pomacanthid care. Its requirements with regard to water quality are not very high, and the fish, acquired as a juvenile, soon begins to eat any kind of food you give it. It is a good

An adult Cortez Angelfish, *Pomacanthus zonipectus,* from Sonora, Mexico. Photo by Alex Kerstitch.

A very young *Pomacanthus zonipectus* (about 2.5 inches). Photo by Alex Kerstitch.

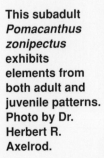

This subadult *Pomacanthus zonipectus* exhibits elements from both adult and juvenile patterns. Photo by Dr. Herbert R. Axelrod.

idea to provide many hiding places, for *Pomacanthus semicirculatus* is an extremely reclusive angelfish. With its maximum length of 16 inches, it is suitable for the aquaria holding 250 gallons or more.

The adult coloration of this species is not very appealing, and adults may become extremely aggressive, especially toward other large angelfishes and other tankmates of similar coloration. Care in reef aquarium is only conditionally recommended, for as the fish ages it may well begin to attack the invertebrates.

GENUS: *PYGOPLITES*

PYGOPLITES DIACANTHUS (BODDART, 1772)

Regal Angelfish; Peacock Angelfish

This book's final report on angelfishes treats the Regal Angelfish, *Pygoplites diacanthus*, which has long been the only species in the genus *Pygoplites*. The description of *Pygoplites diacanthus* has been left for last, although according to listing criteria it really should have appeared between *Apolemichthys* and *Chaetodontoplus*. I left it until last because of the extreme difficulty associated with its care, which made me wonder if it should be included at all. But because this species shows up on the market relatively frequently, I decided to include a description of it in this book.

Even the size of the animal as it appears on the market makes it unsuitable for aquarium care. The fish are usually half grown and so far along in their feeding specialization that getting them to accept a substitute diet is almost never successful. It appears that *Pygoplites diacanthus* begins to eat a specialized diet when it is quite small, which means that if you acquire a Regal Angelfish 2.4 to 3.2 inches long, you are already dealing with a feeding specialist.

It is no wonder, then, that during the first few weeks in aquarium care, 90 percent of imported *Pygoplites diacanthus* starve to death. If you have ever watched a fish slowly die from starvation, you will certainly never forget it. First, the fish grows a little thinner every day; the process is barely perceptible. But then, after a few days, it speeds up. The flanks cave in, then the pointed backbone appears, a sure sign that the fish is beyond saving. This usually happens after you have had it for

Pygoplites diacanthus is one of the most beautiful of the large angelfishes, but it is also one of the most difficult to keep. It is recommended only for the most experienced aquarists. Photo by Günter Speis.

about two weeks. A short time later the Regal Angelfish is so emaciated that it has difficulty keeping its balance. Swimming is reduced to a small circle—the fish is really just staying in one place. It no longer notices its surroundings. Finally, after about three weeks, the fish finally collapses. Lying on its side on the bottom, the fish is so weak that it cannot even defend itself against the little bottom crustaceans that crawl over it incessantly. Nor can the Regal Angelfish protect itself from other tankmates, which now begin to finish it off. Sand that has been stirred up falls slowly on the fish lying flat on the bottom, which, in its struggle against death, tries vainly to right itself—but it is no use. Again and again, the bottom draws the fish to it like a magnet. It stares at its keeper in silent reproach. The fish usually dies the following night.

It is doubtful that this is your goal when you entertain the wish to acquire a feeding specialist, and I certainly do not recommend it just to satisfy your own ego. Marine aquarists should

help protect life, not wipe it out.

There are always exceptions, of course, and *Pygoplites diacanthus* that are less than 2 inches long may become adjusted to life in the aquarium of an experienced marine aquarist. Requirements are excellent water conditions, an abundance of hiding places, a few, not very lively, tankmates, and a natural aquarium setting. Reef aquaria have proven to be good environments. But I should mention that a number of soft corals, gorgonians, leather corals, sponges, crustose anemones, clams, and sometimes even disk anemones will be damaged or even eaten completely. There are great differences in this regard from individual to individual.

Until the fish accepts a substitute diet, sessile invertebrates are a life-saving transitional food, with algae, sponges, and the small crustaceans living in the tank as supplements. The best way to get it to accept a substitute diet is to offer mussels or heart clams in their shell. These shellfish should be bought fresh from the market or grocery store.

Once *Pygoplites diacanthus* accepts food offered to it, the palette can be expanded to include *Artemia* and *Mysis*. There are also reports that feeding *Pygoplites diacanthus* will also take dried food.

Pygoplites that have started to eat may stop again if they suffer a sudden, severe disturbance, for example if a larger fish, or other fish that *Pygoplites diacanthus* chases, is added to the tank. Among such fishes are also small species such as some dwarf groupers. Under no circumstances should other large angelfishes be kept in the same aquarium with *Pygoplites diacanthus*, for the latter will often react in unforeseeable ways. It frequently stops eating, especially if other angelfishes are added to the tank and turn out to be feeding competitors, which actually is always the case.

Pygoplites also react sensitively to a sudden deterioration of water quality, so it is important to have the best technical equipment possible and, above all, avoid putting too many fish in the tank.

If you have the opportunity to get several *Pygoplites diacanthus* in the recommended size, you absolutely should do it, for such a situation is extremely favorable for the fish's well-being; an aquarium holding at least 180 gallons is essential. If you meet these requirements, you will see that the Regal Angelfish has considerably fewer problems during the acclimatization phase. There is still the danger, however, that a large number of the invertebrates will fall victim to the fish.

Juveniles of *Pygoplites diacanthus* differ only slightly from adults, which lack only the eyespot typical of juveniles.

Until recently, it was thought that *Pygoplites diacanthus* was quite rare, but we now know that the species is rather common at depths of between 40 and 65 feet.

One peculiarity of *Pygoplites diacanthus* is its habit of always keeping its belly toward the bottom, which means that, from its hiding place, it can suddenly be looking out at its keeper upside down. Even more reclusive than the adults are the juveniles, which is probably why young Regal Angelfish are only sporadically imported.

Males of *Pygoplites diacanthus* develop large territories in which several females live; these females are only slightly aggressive toward others of the same species and sex, which means that the Regal Angelfish is also found on the reef in groups of

Young *Pygoplites diacanthus* have a color pattern similar to that of adults. Photo by Dr. Herbert R. Axelrod.

three to five animals.

The coloration of this angelfish, which grows to 10 inches, is variable, and primarily dependent on the region the fish came from. Animals from the Maldives have a yellow chest, those from the Red Sea a reddish one, and those from Indonesia a white one. This does not have anything to do with difficulty of care, although there are reports calling attention to the fact that white-chested species adapt most readily to aquarium life. The reason for this, however, may be that the white-chested variety is the most common.

In conclusion, I note that, in principle, *Pygoplites diacanthus* is unsuited for aquarium life and really should be eliminated from dealers' order lists. Where there is no demand, there is no supply.

SUMMARY

One of the most beautiful of the angelfishes is *Pygoplites diacanthus*. But it is also one of the most difficult to care for and is only suitable for life in an aquarium if the tank contains many invertebrates and the Regal Angelfish is not larger than 2 inches. During care, the keeper must do without a number of invertebrates—the ones *Pygoplites diacanthus* has helped itself to.

Requirements for care include excellent water parameters, maintained by a good technical setup, and—very important—not too many fishes in the tank. Furthermore, you must do without fishes that compete with the Regal Angelfish for food. The primary competitors are large angelfishes introduced later into the tank.

Until the fish finally begins to eat a substitute diet in the form of fresh mussels and heart shells, invertebrates (especially small crustaceans) and algae are essential for life. Once a substitute diet has been accepted, *Artemia* and *Mysis* can be added successfully. A few individuals accept flake food.

It is a good idea to keep *Pygoplites diacanthus* in a group of 3 to 5 individuals in a reef aquarium holding at least 180 gallons. This situation corresponds most closely to natural conditions, makes the fish a little less shy, and awakens its curiosity about new kinds of food. This is no guarantee that the fish will eat, however.

The Regal Angelfish, *Pygoplites diacanthus*, belongs in the hands of very experienced marine aquarists. Nevertheless, common sense says that, for the good of the fish, importation and aquarium care should be stopped.

SEX-RELATED CHARACTERISTICS, PAIR FORMATION, AND MATING BEHAVIOR

This chapter is one of the most difficult because it deals with a subject that has been understood for only a short time, and has not been studied adequately by scientists. Although it has become increasingly possible in recent years to raise in dry-land aquaria the various species of *Amphiprion*, sea horses, pipefishes, and, just recently, dwarf groupers and pitmakers, the subject of this chapter is still extremely problematic for many coral fishes. It is particularly difficult when the spawn consists of pelagic eggs. Before you get fertilized eggs, however, you have to have one male and one female of a species—in short, a pair. Certainly the worst way to do this is to catch a pair in its native habitat, right from the reef, with intent to keep them in an aquarium. Marine aquarists suggest that a much better way is to let young animals grow into sexually mature pairs, which will then release eggs and sperm in the aquarium. In attempting this, make sure to observe the natural prerequisites for pair formation.

For marine angelfishes there is the harem structure, already discussed, which consists of one male and several ranked females. There is a difference between true and false harems. The true harem, as practiced by the dwarf or pygmy angelfishes, for example, presumes that one male has several females. They all swim around in a group, crisscrossing the territory of the male fish.

A false harem, as found, for example, in many large angelfishes, also presumes one male and several females. But the females show no established hierarchy. Each female of a false harem has her own territory within that of the male. If one of the harem females does not observe the territorial boundaries of another, the intruder is fiercely driven off. This form of harem explains why many species of *Pomacanthus*, for example, are considered today to be solitary and are seldom observed as a pair.

PAIR FORMATION IN *CENTROPYGE*

If you look at pair formation in the genus of the smallest marine angelfishes, the pygmy angelfishes, the problems posed here are easy to solve.

Like *Amphiprion*, many species of the genus *Centropyge* undergo sex change. The largest, strongest animal becomes the male, and the rest remain females. Reversing the process, changing from male back to female, seems no longer possible according to investigations conducted to date.

In the wild, many species of pygmy angelfishes live in true harems. If the male is removed, in two or three weeks the highest-ranking female will turn into a functional male and take over leadership of the harem. Any color variations that may sometimes occur do not appear for another few months to two years.

In the marine aquarium hobby, consequently, it is the practice to introduce one large pygmy angelfish and several smaller ones of the same species into the aquarium at the same time. Naturally, a prerequisite is a large aquarium with plenty of hiding places, where the weaker animals can withdraw from power struggles at first. After about two weeks roles are established, and from then on the pygmy angelfishes will maintain their positions.

After a while, under good aquarium conditions, the pygmy angelfishes will spawn. You should know, however, that this happens frequently in reef aquaria but has only seldom been observed in fish aquaria.

Actual spawning takes place in the evening, when the only light in the reef aquarium is the blue one, and only for another hour. Mating begins with the male's courtship. First, he flares his dorsal fin, at the same time turning his flank toward the female, swimming around her while drifting toward the surface. This goes on until the female follows him. Then the male carefully approaches the underside of her body and begins touching her belly with his head, at the same time forcing her upward toward the surface. On the way up, the male suddenly turns so that the two sexes are swimming belly to belly toward the surface. Once they have reached the highest point of their territory, the two animals shoot apart. Either sperm and eggs are released at that point or the sequence described is repeated. You know spawning has been successful when you see a white cloud that rapidly disperses in the current. This cloud consists of, among other things, a few hundred thousand eggs; after 24 to 48 hours, depending on the temperature of the water, the microscopic larvae hatch.

For the next few days the larvae feed on their yolk sack, until their eyes and gut, including the mouth, have developed. And this is where the aquarist's problems begin, for the difficulty of providing a suitable food in sufficient quantity has not yet been resolved. In addition, rearing some larvae is made more difficult by the fact that the snapping reflex is triggered only by plankton that move in a certain way, for example extremely suddenly.

PAIR FORMATION IN *GENICANTHUS*

In many species of the genus *Genicanthus*, pair formation is similar to that in the pygmy angelfishes. In addition to sex change, which has been scientifically documented, there is a sex-related difference in coloration.

In nature, species of the genus *Genicanthus* live mostly in small groups which also adhere to the true harem structure.

The lyretail angelfish genus is one of those about whose lifestyle little is known. So it is impossible to report on courting and spawning behavior in detail, for, to date, no aquarium observations exist.

PAIR FORMATION IN *CHAETODONTOPLUS* AND *APOLEMICHTHYS*

Although the aquarium hobby has turned up some information about *Apolemichthys* and *Chaetodontoplus*, courtship and spawning behavior are still a mystery, having not been observed to date.

All we know about *Apolemichthys trimaculatus* is that the species prefers the false harem structure. Within the territory of a male *Apolemichthys trimaculatus* are the defined territories of its female counterparts.

In some species of *Chaetodontoplus*, for example *C. dubouleyi*, different sex-specific color variations are known. Males have a distinct white spot behind the eye; in females the mark is sketchy.

Some species of the genus *Chaetodontoplus* live on the reef in pairs.

PAIR FORMATION IN *PYGOPLITES*

For the three genera of marine angelfishes just described, little is known about their sexual behavioral roles, but for *Pygoplites diacanthus* a number of observations have been published.

The Regal Angelfish also lives in territories, but for a long time it was not known whether *Pygoplites diacanthus* had a true or false harem structure. It is likely, and various observations support this, that both forms appear. *Pygoplites diacanthus* has been observed to be solitary, to live in pairs, and even in groups of three to five animals.

As already described under aquarium care, several different-size individuals should be kept. All of the Regal Angelfish should be placed in the tank at the same time, and there should be no more than five.

Little has been published about courtship and spawning behavior in *Pygoplites diacanthus*. From a publication by Dr. R. Thresher, we know that the Regal Angelfish, like all pomacanthids, spawns at the uppermost point of its territory. Eggs and sperm are released free into the water.

PAIR FORMATION IN *HOLACANTHUS*

In recent years, much new information has appeared about the remaining genera of marine angelfishes described in this book. According to what we know now, most species of the genus *Holacanthus* organize false harems.

Here, too, males are generally larger than females. For marine aquarists, however, this is not much of a clue, for the fish should be acquired at a young age. Spawning takes place at dusk at the uppermost point in a territory.

Recently, the capacity for sex change has been demonstrated for *Holacanthus tricolor*. Here, too, females can turn into males. For the rest of the species of *Holacanthus*, however, this has not been demonstrated, at least with regard to adults. To date, no studies have been made to find out whether juveniles change sex before they take on adult coloration, but such a change cannot be ruled out.

In addition to being able to change sex, mature individuals of *Holacanthus tricolor* also show a phenotypic difference, which, however, is not very apparent. Males have a few pale red spots on the tail fin; females lack these.

In the aquarium, pair formation for *Holacanthus tricolor* is quite easy to bring about. You put two or three juveniles of the species all at once into a sufficiently large aquarium. If the aquarium is too small, the animals may become quarrelsome with one another as they grow.

Another method for successful pair formation in species of *Holacanthus* as well as *Pomacanthus* is the following:

First, the aquarist gets an animal in juvenile coloration. As mentioned in the description of the species, under good conditions the fish will take on adult coloration after a while. You wait, then, until your animal has its adult colors. The fact that this may take two years should not stand in your way. Once this goal has been achieved, you can add a juvenile of the same species without any concern at all. As already related, adults do not normally attack the differently colored juveniles.

During the year following the acquisition of a second animal, the process of pair formation proceeds like this:

After a certain time, the juvenile begins to change color. With the transformation to adult coloration, the fish also assumes the sex that is required to form a pair with the fish of its species that is already in the aquarium. Meanwhile, sex change has already been scientifically documented for juveniles of some species as well.

There is another possibility for pairing species of *Holacanthus* and *Pomacanthus* successfully, and it takes a lot less time. Get two different-size juveniles of one species at the same time. Put them both into the aquarium you have set up for them. It is important that the aquarium is large and has an abundance of hiding places, so that the two animals can stay out of each other's way. Friction may well develop and is thoroughly normal; it will stop after two or three weeks. Whether these conflicts are necessary to establish sexual identity remains to be investigated.

There is yet another way to form a pair. For either *Pomacanthus* or *Holacanthus*, get one juvenile and one adult. The procedure is like the one just described.

Because of the attendant problems already described with regard to adding individuals in adult coloration, you should not use this method. An exception to this method is provided by species of the genus *Euxiphipops*, for here the fish take on adult coloration when they are quite small, less than 4 inches long. Put an adult-colored *Euxiphipops* and a juvenile, or a fish in transitional coloration, into the tank at the same time. Be careful— do not add a small fish in adult coloration. This simply will not work!

PAIR FORMATION IN *POMACANTHUS*

Some of the information about pair formation in *Pomacanthus* has already been covered in the description of *Holacanthus*, for the two genera have much in common. However, in recent years, there have been many observations of spawning behavior in *Pomacanthus*.

Most species of *Pomacanthus* live in false harems. *Pomacanthus paru* is an exception; on the reef it is found mostly in pairs and even in groups of up to twenty individuals.

Species of *Pomacanthus* spawn at certain times of the year at dusk at the uppermost point in the female's territory. Theoretically, the aquarium should be about 30 feet high if an adult pair of *Pomacanthus imperator* is to spawn. This theoretical height is important because the difference in pressure is important: as the female rises to the surface, the genital papillae expand to the point that the eggs can be released.

The most important detail is the size of the spawning pair. Because only young animals should be kept, the issue of size is unavoidable. In a normal reef aquarium, large marine angelfishes are not as big as they would be in their natural reef habitat; as a result, conditions for successful spawning are different. That spawning up to a certain size under suitable conditions will in fact take place is evidenced by care of species of the genus *Centropyge*.

Sex-related characters in species of *Pomacanthus* vary and may be categorized, as will now be described for *Pomacanthus imperator*.

It is known that a number of *Pomacanthus* are able to make clicking sounds. In pairs of *Pomacanthus imperator* it can be determined that the sounds differ considerably in loudness from one sex to the other. But the clicking sounds made by juvenile forms of *Pomacanthus imperator* and *Euxiphipops navarchus* also differ; each specimen has its specific sound pattern.

Consequently, we cannot rule out that each specimen, or at least each species, has its own pattern of clicking sounds at each stage of its development. The sound is produced by a rib, called a functional rib, that is moved by a specially developed muscle; as the muscle expands and contracts, the rib strikes the swim bladder. The swim bladder serves as a soundboard; the audible clicking sound is produced by the functional rib beating on the swim bladder. Because special equipment is required to evaluate the sounds picked up in order to translate the audible sound to a visual interpretation, this method is reserved for scientific institutions.

The situation is different for particular behavioral patterns, those typical of both sexes and those typical of one or the other.

Submissive behavior is expressed primarily by the male *Pomacanthus imperator*. At the approach of a stronger female animal, a male of the same species will first fold its tail fin. Then comes a contraction of the soft-rayed dorsal and anal fins.

Pomacanthus imperator make clicking sounds, with the sounds differing in loudness from one sex to the other. However, even juveniles make distinctive clicking sounds. Photo by Roger Steene.

Finally, the white facial mask turns black.

The color change in the facial mask is not specific to males but has been observed in female animals as well, as in when the fish takes on its sleeping coloration after dark,

Pomacanthus imperator spawns at certain times of the year at dusk at the highest point of the female's territory. Photo by Roger Steene.

or when *Pomacanthus imperator* is unwell. The folding of the tail fin, however, occurs only in dominant animals and has not been observed in females. Submissive behavior is more commonly practiced by subordinate members of a species, when one adult approaches another. In the natural habitat, submissive behavior is used by males to gain entry to the territory of a female that is ready to spawn.

Certainly, the blue forehead spots observed on some adults of *Pomacanthus imperator* are not a sex-specific character. Rather, they are a remnant of the juvenile coloration; as the fish ages, the spots disappear. This has been observed by B. Conde, director of the Zoological Institute in Nancy, France, among others.

With a presentation of sex-specific characters of marine angelfishes and pair formation, this book comes to an end. I hope I have been able to persuade marine aquarists to keep more pairs in their aquaria in the future.

Many unanswered questions remain that deserve answers. Frequently, observations made by marine aquarists—amateur marine biologists—contribute to explanations of scientific questions, or at least to shedding light on various problems. The reverse is also possible, of course: the observations of marine aquarists raise questions for which answers must then be found.

I am certain that one day pelagic spawners, and this includes members of the marine angelfish family, will be raised successfully in the aquarium. If this book succeeds in inspiring marine aquarists to become more active in the species-specific care, pair formation, spawning, and rearing of coral reef fishes, it will have achieved its goal.